# Living Large
## IN OUR LITTLE HOUSE

# Living Large
## IN OUR LITTLE HOUSE

Thriving in **480** Square Feet with Six Dogs, a Husband,
and One Remote—Plus More Stories of How You Can Too

Our little house

**KERRI FIVECOAT-CAMPBELL**

Foreword by Kent Griswold
of the *Tiny House Blog*

**Reader's** digest | New York / Montreal

Library of Congress Cataloging-in-Publication Data
Names: Fivecoat-Campbell, Kerri, author.
Title: Living large in our little house : thriving in 480-square feet with
    six dogs, a husband and one remote–and more stories of how you can too /
    Kerri Fivecoat-Campbell.
Description: New York : Reader's Digest Association, Inc., 2016. | Includes
    bibliographical references.
Identifiers: LCCN 2016001140 (print) | LCCN 2016001649 (ebook) | ISBN
    9781621452522 (hardback) | ISBN 9781621452539 ()
Subjects: LCSH: Small houses. | Lifestyles. | Fivecoat-Campbell, Kerri. |
    BISAC: BIOGRAPHY & AUTOBIOGRAPHY / Personal Memoirs. | REFERENCE /
    Personal & Practical Guides. | HOUSE & HOME / General.
Classification: LCC NA7533 .F53 2016 (print) | LCC NA7533 (ebook) | DDC
    728/.37–dc23
LC record available at http://lccn.loc.gov/2016001140

We are committed to both the quality of our products and the service we provide to our customers. We value your comments, so please feel free to contact us.

Reader's Digest Trade Publishing
44 South Broadway
White Plains, NY 10601

For more Reader's Digest products and information, visit our website:
www.rd.com (in the United States)

Printed in China

10 9 8 7 6 5 4 3 2 1

For Dale, my best friend and soul mate:
I hope we have many more years of Living Large together.

And for Steffi, Meg-Ann, Sofia, and Millie: I'm so happy for the privilege of
being your American mom and grandma. May you always Live Large,
no matter where life takes you—xoxo.

# Contents

# Foreword

I first met Kerri Fivecoat-Campbell through the Tiny House Blog. She initially contacted me with an idea about sharing her story of living in her small cabin in the woods. She had the writing chops to tackle Living Large in Our Little House, but wanted me to help her reach the growing tiny house audience.

Up to that point, I had mainly concentrated on different types of structures that could be built and lived in, and there had not been many stories about those who were actually living this lifestyle.

Kerri had the vision to take it to the next level, providing a new angle of sharing her experiences living her life full-time in a little house.

Kerri changed the landscape online, sharing her life, including both the good and the struggles of living in a little home. Through her blog, she developed a following of those interested in living the tiny and little house life. Kerri has done an excellent job in the blogosphere, interacting and developing a true sense of community on Living Large in Our Little House.

Through her example I even started to change the direction of the Tiny House Blog to include stories of other people living in tiny and small homes.

This book not only expands on Kerri and Dale's story and how they ended up in their little house, but it also brings to life some of the stories of the other community members who call the Living Large blog and Facebook page home.

The joys of downsizing are many. Most tiny house dwellers live debt-free. They enjoy more of life, often working from home as entrepreneurs because they are able to live on less. They have less stuff to manage and more time for their passions. But the little and tiny house life isn't always rosy, and Living Large in Our Little House eloquently describes the challenges, allowing new little house dwellers to avoid the same mistakes.

Kerri speaks of the pioneers of the movement, but she has also become a pioneer herself, forging ahead and clearing the path for new people to the movement, helping them navigate building restrictions and code requirements as well as the lifestyle.

I know you will enjoy Kerri's writing and, like me, won't want to put the book down. Thank you, Kerri, for sharing your story with us.

Kent Griswold
Editor/Owner, Tiny House Blog

# Acknowledgments

How do you thank the universe? Literally, I feel like I have the universe to thank for putting me in the right place at the right time to learn how to Live Large by having less.

I also have a universe full of support from friends, colleagues and loved ones:

My husband, Dale, has been there for me through thick and thin, through the angst of my teens, now to menopause. He's always supported and encouraged me in my writing and for that, I'm truly grateful.

This whole adventure would not have been possible without my aunt Kathy and Monty, who gave us this gift of paradise in the Ozarks. Thank you, too, for helping us design Our Little House.

A note of gratitude to our builder, Terry Young: Our Little House is as solid as your construction knowledge and principles.

My agent, Marilyn Allen, who heard an unorganized pitch one rainy day in New York and worked with me for literally several years to develop a cohesive book idea. Thank you for your enthusiasm for this project and never giving up.

To my editors at Reader's Digest, Andrea Au Levitt and Amy Reilly, who polished the manuscript and kept it on point.

A big thank you to Kent Griswold, who has always so generously answered my questions, helped me meet people within the tiny/small house movement and who didn't hesitate when asked to write the foreword for this book.

A big shout out and thanks goes out to everyone who participated in this book by telling their stories and sharing the photos of their beautiful tiny/small homes. A special note of gratitude to Sue Smith Moak, who wanted to continue to share her story in memory of her husband, Rick, who was so excited about seeing their home profiled in this book. Unfortunately, he won't get to see it, but I'm sure Sue's perseverance at the ranch is making his spirit proud.

I am lucky to have some really good friends who are always there for me, sometimes on a daily basis, when I need to talk or get their thoughts on something I've written: Kathleen Winn, Terri Onorato, Barb Vatza, and Allie Johnson, thank you all for being my rocks and my cheerleaders, but most of all, thank you for being my dose of reality when I need it.

To my colleagues, Vera Badertsher, Jane Boursaw, Alisa Bowman, Roxanne Hawn, Sandy Grabbe, Donna Hull, Claudine Jalajas, Sheryl Kraft, Jennifer Margulis, Melanie McMinn, Ruth Pennebaker, Meredith Resnick, Brette Sember, Kris Bordessa, and Stephanie Stiavetti, thank you all for being with me through the development and evolution of my blog. You all are such an awesome group of women!

My appreciation to my longtime friend, Aaron Hopkins, for redesigning the Living Large logo for the blog and Facebook page and to my blog designer, Charles Parnell, for putting together a great blog design. Kevin Pieper, it's always great when you photograph our home. Kudos to Kali Hostetler, who did my hair and make-up for the photos in the book, you are a talented lady.

My appreciation to Beverly Blair Harzog, Janine Adams, Irene Levine, and Sarah Susanka for being expert resources. The generous sharing of your time is so greatly appreciated.

Of course, I would be remiss as a Dog Mom for not thanking my admin team that accompanies me to my Belle Writer's Studio every day, providing me with comic relief, thoughtful reflection, writing fodder and some slobbery dog kisses when needed; our 5 lovely rescued (recycled) dogs, Dakota, Sade, Chloe, Abbi, and Dexter. Hershey, Emma and Molly, and our cats, Cali and Tabitha, though no longer with us in the physical world, will always be a part of our hearts at Our Little House.

I would like to thank our friends and family who have braved the wilds of the Ozark Mountains (and the threat of banjos) to come and share with us our Living Large experience: Mike and Charlotte Bixler, Jennifer Dearing, Philip Hendrix, Lora Carr, Shelly Grauberger, Shelby Mata, Frank and Barb Burton, Bob and Dee Campbell, and Kathleen and David Winn. Our house would not quite be a home without your visits.

Finally, thank you to the entire Living Large in Our Little House blog and Facebook community for reading, sharing your experiences, and making this book possible.

# Living Large

## IN OUR LITTLE HOUSE

# 1

# From the Wilson House
# to Our Little House:
## How We Discovered
## the Tiny House Movement

*Living Truth: One of my favorite quotes is from the song "Beautiful Boy" by John Lennon: "Life is what happens to you while you're busy making other plans."*

## July 1984

Golden rays of a setting July sun beamed through leaded-glass windows, highlighting dancing dust particles in the air. It was the only movement in what had been a bustling and busy family home until just a few hours before. My mother and sister had taken their last loads of belongings, but I was still working on getting mine out. After I finished, Mom asked me to return to the empty 1920s Tudor to do one more walk-through and leave the keys and a note on the kitchen counter for the people who had purchased what had once been her dream house.

I was twenty years old and excited to be moving into my first apartment, but also a little scared to be on my own. When it was just me and those scattering dust particles, I felt a sharp pang of loneliness. I walked through the house, my footsteps echoing on the polished wood floors. Just five years earlier, my mom had finally realized her dream of restoring a historic home in our blue-collar neighborhood of Turner, a once rural township incorporated in the 1960s into Kansas City, Kansas.

## April 1979

In their mid-fifties, my parents were upsizing from an 800-square-foot stucco bungalow to the 1,800-square-foot brick Tudor. It had taken thirty-four years, but they were finally making it out of their starter home. They were living *the* American Dream.

Our community was a working-class railroad community—the railroads ran right through the end of town. In fact, the name "Turner" is believed to have originated from when railroad men to the east were switching the direction of a train and would say, "Turn her around!" Most men in Turner either worked at the railroad, like my father, or at one of the many businesses that supported the railroad, like my father-in-law, who worked for a company that made wheels for railroad cars.

My dad, Frank Fivecoat, hard at work at the Santa Fe Railroad.

By the standards of our largely working-class community, the brick home with a red clay–tile roof was a mansion. It was built by prominent turn-of-the-century town banker and grocer Charles S. Wilson for his wife, Nannie, and was known as the Wilson House. It had a one-car garage, a mudroom, a large country kitchen, and a spacious dining room with a built-in china cabinet. The living room also had built-in bookcases flanking the fireplace. The original leaded-glass doors and windows were still intact. Beautiful French doors of the same high-quality woodwork that was throughout the rest of the home led to a four-season porch. Surprisingly, the home also retained all of its original light fixtures, including several small crystal chandeliers in the living and dining rooms.

The once meticulously cared for three-quarter-acre corner lot had plenty of bushes providing privacy from the street, as well as the remnants of a small fish pond and a magnolia tree, which was uncommon that far north.

The Wilson House, the 1920s Tudor that represented my parents' version of the American Dream.

When my parents purchased it in 1979, the home had most recently been used as a rental. It had been abused and neglected. The leaded glass was cloudy with dust and dirt, and the wood floors were covered with hideous green shag carpet. The textured plaster walls weren't painted to highlight the meticulous craftsmanship, and some of the walls were actually a deep purple. As a 15-year-old, I viewed it as an old house that had seen better days. But my parents, especially my mother, who had always been creative, recognized that there was beauty under all that dirt and neglect.

When my mom and dad first told me we were moving into the Wilson House, I was horrified. Not only were we leaving our perfect little bungalow for that old, filthy building, but they were also moving us to our community's rumored haunted house. Every town has one, and the Wilson House was ours. The book and movie *The Amityville Horror* was popular at the time, and the Wilson House reminded me of the fabled haunted home where demons supposedly compelled a young man to slaughter his entire family.

I loved our little bungalow. When Dad took a job as a car inspector for the railroad in the late '40s, my parents bought it new for under $10,000. Over the years, they made substantial renovations to create the perfect home. They transformed the one-car garage into additional space for the living room. A third bedroom for my older brother and a family room with a fireplace eventually became part of the house. My mom quickly learned the value of having built-ins in a small home. During the renovations, she added plenty of built-in cabinets and shelves to give us more space for our stuff. Still, the home was less than 1,000 square feet.

By the time I came along in my parents' midlife, seven of us shared the little abode, including my three teenage siblings (two sisters and a brother) and ailing grandmother. My grandmother passed away when I was still a baby, and by the time I was 6, my older siblings had left the nest, leaving me with a bedroom to myself. My brother Steve did move back home after returning from the military, but Mom had already converted his room into a sewing room. Steve worked long night shifts at an automobile manufacturing plant, and when he was home, he slept on a hide-a-bed in the family room.

We were part of a group of tightly knit, longtime residents on the block that included my godparents. Many of them were railroad families, but there were also firefighters, teachers, and factory workers. It was the type of place where kids could ride their bikes up and down the street and play until the street lamps came on or our mothers stepped onto the stoop to call us home.

Though the Wilson House was just across town, we didn't know anyone well in our new neighborhood. The house was also enormous compared to the space we'd had in our small bungalow, and I felt lost walking through it for the first time. Although I had an entire third-floor bedroom bigger than some studio apartments—and my own bathroom—my love for the old Tudor was not as immediate as my mother's.

Like most teenagers, I was pretty self-absorbed and cared only that my life was being interrupted. I tried to protest our move once when I was alone with my father. "Dad, I really don't want to move to that old house. It's huge, and everyone says it's haunted. . . . It's not home."

My dad sighed. He didn't come from an era when kids had a say in decisions reserved for adults. "Now look here," he began in his Arkansas drawl. "Your mother wants this, and I want to give it to her. Look at the space you'll have in that bedroom. It will feel like home in no time." What Dad lacked in his physical stature was made up for in his stern presence. I knew that was the end of that conversation.

He was right, of course. My parents spent every free moment that summer ripping up the old carpet, stripping hardwood floors, painting, polishing long-neglected chandeliers and leaded glass, and choosing drapes and carpet for the living room. It didn't look at all like the decrepit, dirty house with purple walls of my first tour. It was a total restoration, and the house shined.

Moving day, however—right before school started at the beginning of August—was a nightmare. My mom was a collector, and it was amazing how much stuff had been stored in our small bungalow. It became a family joke that everything from their 34-year marriage (including an empty laundry-detergent box full of dryer lint) was moved that day.

My mom, dad, and I spent the first night in our new home sleeping on the four-season porch, as the central air had yet to be installed and it was very hot in the house. It was a rare treat for us to be together for an entire evening, since my dad also worked a second full-time job as a night security guard. My parents seemed downright giddy that night, and we laughed and talked until we drifted to sleep, like teenagers at a slumber party.

My third-floor room *was* awesome. I got a new brass bed and matching entertainment center, dresser, and desk. I had two huge closets (including a cedar closet to store my off-season clothes), my own bathroom (no more sharing with my parents or Steve), and a bonus area off of my bathroom in the unfinished attic to store more stuff. And store more stuff I did. I put boxes of childhood memories in that area. My bedroom was filled in no time, as was the attic storage area.

My bedroom was large enough for a sitting area, and I had my own small couch with a foldout bed. When I asked my parents if we could host an exchange student that year, it took little convincing, since we had the room. Angela Henderson, who lived near Melbourne, Australia, joined our family not long after we moved in. That fulfilled a dream of mine too; I finally had a sibling closer to my age.

Angela wasn't the only one to join our household. After graduating from high school that spring, Dale, my high school sweetheart, needed someplace to live. His mother had sold her home, and he had just found a union job with a meat company but didn't yet have money saved for his own place. He had been staying on his aunt and uncle's couch. Although we had only been dating a short time, my parents really liked Dale, so he moved into the basement with Steve. With Mom at home and Dale working nights, we were sternly cautioned not to try any "funny business." It would have been hard, even if either of us had gotten up the courage to sneak between floors, since the renovation hadn't done anything to correct those squeaking stairs.

Here I am with Angela Henderson (left) and with Dale in September 1979, three months after we met.

Life was much different than it had been in the little bungalow, where we were often mere steps from each other at any given time. In the brick Tudor, we all had not only our own space but also really, our own floors. Mom read in the living room, worked restoring all of the gardens, or hung out in the master bedroom, which was large enough to double as a sewing room. Dad had his garage, and Steve and Dale hung out in the basement family room with the home's only cable-connected television.

My room on the third floor gave me the freedom to play my stereo louder than I could have in the bungalow, something I valued greatly because there were no iPods or earbuds at that time. Steve, a child of the '50s and '60s, instilled in me a love of rock and roll. I dreamed of becoming a writer—a rock and roll journalist for *Rolling Stone*.

During our first Christmas in the Wilson House, my parents held an open house, proudly showing off the newly renovated home to family and friends. Mom reveled in decorating the house for holidays. She put our large family tree on the four-season porch and put a smaller tree for their five grandsons in the living room. We were, in that first year, one big happy family.

The dining room, kitchen, and living room of the Wilson House, with the original fixtures lovingly restored by my parents.

I knew little of my parents' finances, but I was aware that it had been a stretch for them to buy and restore the home. In that first year, they had also opened a store that sold handcrafted goods my mother and others made, which stretched their finances even further. Mom was very talented and creative, and she hoped to build a business that could take them into retirement. However, it takes time to build a business and draw a profit, and time was something my parents weren't aware that they didn't have.

Soon after Angela returned to Australia, things began to go awry. My father had suffered a heart attack several years before and also had diabetes. Both my dad and Steve, a veteran of the Vietnam War, were "functioning alcoholics," which meant we knew they had an alcohol problem, but for the most part, that didn't interfere with their daily lives or ability to work. My father was a good, loving dad and had always provided for his family. His drinking only became a problem when he wasn't working. Steve had more difficulty controlling his addiction.

My father's health began to deteriorate—most likely from the combination of the physical demands of working two full-time jobs, his increased drinking, and his uncontrolled diabetes. Typically an easygoing man, his behavior at times became erratic and out of character. He once walked out of a grocery store completely unaware that he had not paid for his items and then got into a verbal altercation with the store's owner when he was confronted. Not long after that he got into another altercation with a superior at his night security job and was fired.

Around the same time, Steve also lost his job at the automobile manufacturing plant and moved out. Then Dale moved out to live with and help his grandmother. The loss of the second income from Dad's night job and the room and board Steve and Dale were paying placed significant financial strain on my parents.

I knew they were having problems, especially after my dad lost his second job. When I was in high school, I worked full-time during the summer and snuck groceries into the house when my dad wasn't home. He was a proud man, and I knew he would be embarrassed if he knew his teenage daughter was using the income from her job at Tasty Queen to help out.

We had only been living in the Wilson House for two years when my dad felt chest pains and was rushed to the hospital, where he died of a massive heart attack, the condition known as "the widow maker." My mom and I went into preservation mode, and life became all about saving the house. I had one year of high school to finish. The money my mom collected in survivor's benefits for me from Railroad Retirement (she was not yet old enough to draw her own retirement) was more than I could earn working a minimum-wage job, so there was no thought of me leaving school. However, my dreams of going to journalism school were put on hold. My high school counselor and Mom decided it would be better for me to enroll in a business program at a community college. I could continue to live at home, and my Railroad Retirement benefits would continue paying my mom's mortgage, instead of for an apartment or a dorm.

My older sister, Janet, and her two sons, Keith and Shawn, moved into the basement so we could all pool our money and combine living expenses. Nearly every penny all of us earned (except what I needed for college tuition), along with my survivor's benefits from Railroad Retirement, went into the mortgage payment, utilities, food, and loans my parents had taken out to start the craft business.

## July 1984

Exactly five years after moving in—almost to the day—I found myself watching those dust particles scattering as my family was scattered throughout Kansas City. Mom knew she couldn't handle that huge home alone and had finally admitted the house was too much for her to maintain, both financially and physically. She went to live the next few years with relatives. Janet was planning to remarry, and she and her children were moving in with her new husband. I was still in college, and my future was yet to be determined. Except for the day of my father's funeral, I had never seen my mother as sad as when she handed me those keys and the note for the new owners.

I went back to my new apartment that night, no longer excited, but heartbroken. What was left of my childhood had shattered the night my father passed away, and if I had any idealistic thoughts left of the American Dream, they were marred by my mother having to give up on hers. Although my mom sold the Wilson House and was able to pay off her bills from the sale, she always felt as though she'd lost the house, because she had never really wanted to move.

My sadness over my mother having to sell her home were mixed with my anxiety over not yet knowing what I wanted to do for a career. My long-term plans had been derailed when it became clear I couldn't attend journalism school. I was still going to business school and working full-time as an assistant manager at the apartment complex I moved to when Mom sold the house. But I knew that wasn't what I wanted to do with my life. I hadn't been ready to leave home—I had hoped to at least finish school and decide on a career before getting my own place. I felt a little cheated that I didn't get to *leave home*. Home had *left me* when it was sold. Not having a home base that I could return to made me feel like I had jumped out of a plane without a parachute.

My parents had worked all their lives to attain that American Dream, and in what seemed like an instant, it was gone. It was a confusing time for me as a young adult. Growing up, my parents had provided me with everything I needed. But I had wanted more *stuff*, so at 14, I began working for family friends at the local Tasty Queen. I wanted my own phone line in my room and designer jeans instead of the less-expensive, department store brands. I ignored my mother's wisdom to just enjoy my youth and worry about working later. It was the '80s, and the message that "bigger is better" was everywhere, from new subdivisions being built around us to the theme song to the sit-com *The Jeffersons*, which pounded into our heads that if we could "move on up," we had arrived.

What did it mean for my mother to have lost that dream? What did it mean for me—and the values my parents instilled in me that, if you worked hard, you were rewarded?

Journey was my favorite band, and the summer my dad passed away, Journey's song, "Don't Stop Believin'" was released. I needed something to tell me things were still going to be okay. The music I loved was at least still a constant in my life; I adopted that song as my life anthem.

I tried to never stop believing that if you work hard, you would be rewarded. Although things went terribly wrong for my mom, I thought being rewarded still meant getting more and bigger. It meant "moving up," but I thought it also meant I had to do it smarter. From the moment I moved from the Wilson House into my one-bedroom apartment at the complex where I was an assistant manager, I felt like I didn't have enough space. What just a few years before would have seemed a huge move up from my tiny bedroom in the bungalow now felt like I had downsized. My bedroom at the Wilson House had been bigger.

Four months after moving to the complex, I moved down the hall to a two-bedroom, so I could set up a spare bedroom and have more room for my two small dogs and two cats.

Dale was also going through a transition that would affect his outlook on jobs and money for the rest of his life. The same summer I moved from the Wilson House into my own apartment, he had lost his union job at the meat company. The workers had gone on strike, and the union was busted. They hired nonunion workers for a fraction of the wages they had been paying the union employees.

Me and my mom, Betty Fivecoat, on my wedding day, July 12, 1986.

Dale took a job at the area's largest landfill as a heavy-equipment operator, but he was only making about half of what he had at the meat company. Losing such a good job shook his confidence; he didn't yet feel comfortable with the commitment of marriage. I also felt it was better for me to live on my own so that I could experience maintaining my own home and budget.

While I lived and worked at the apartment complex, I also went to college and sometimes worked as many as three jobs. By the fall of 1985, Dale and I were ready to try living together before planning for our wedding in the summer of 1986. We moved from our apartments to a two-bedroom duplex with a basement garage. We would make one more move to an even larger duplex apartment before buying our first home.

## New Year's Eve 1989

I could not wait for Dale and I to fulfill our own American Dream and buy a home. After being married for a year, we began looking for houses. It took us two years to agree on a style. We had very different ideas about the type of house we wanted. Initially, I wanted a large Victorian. For someone who at one time did not want to move into a big, older home, I had come to love the idea of restoring something old. I also inherited a love of antiques from Mom. Dale and I even looked at the Wilson House, which had come up for sale during our search, but it was priced beyond our comfort zone.

My parents' experience taught us not to exceed what we felt comfortable paying. We were young, still in our twenties, and not making a lot of money. I was working at a consumer credit card collection facility, and Dale was still driving heavy equipment at the landfill. He liked that he got a lot of overtime each week, and the job seemed layoff-proof. No matter what the economy was doing, the city was always going to have trash.

After looking at older homes, Dale decided he wanted a newer house that didn't need a lot of work and didn't cost a fortune to maintain. He had grown up in a 1960s-style raised ranch, and that's what felt like home to him. We compromised on an 11-year-old, 1,100-square-foot split-level. The house was built in 1979, the year we started dating and the year my family moved to the Wilson House. Superstitious about numbers, I took it as a positive sign. Our split-level had some features I liked in older homes, such as vaulted ceilings, arched entryways, a large country kitchen, and a beautiful brick fireplace in the downstairs family room.

We closed on our first home and moved in on New Year's Eve, 1989.

The New Year of 1990 would begin our journey to our American Dream. By that point, we knew that we didn't want biological children. The three-bedroom, one-and-a-half-bath home with a two-car garage gave us plenty of space for our stuff. We put the second bedroom to use as an office when we got our first computer in 1992. Our third bedroom also served a purpose for two years. Like my parents had welcomed Angela so many years before, we hosted our own two exchange daughters for a year each. It wasn't long, though, before we felt we needed more storage space, and so we built a 10-by-10-foot shed in the backyard.

Dale had always been good at fixing cars. He got a new job at the landfill in the diesel mechanic shop, a move that provided him with a trade and a more secure future. I finally finished my business degree and was also moving up in management at the credit center where I worked, which was affiliated with a large national bank.

Throughout the first 10 years we lived in the split-level, we spent many Sundays going to open houses in new subdivisions, marveling at the huge McMansions with master bedroom/bath suites bigger than our formal living room. On a couple of occasions, we fell in love with a floor plan, talked to the realtor on-site, and tossed around numbers.

The split-level home Dale and I bought on New Year's Eve, 1989.

But it always came down to those numbers. Our incomes were moving up, so weren't we supposed to move up with them? We didn't, however, want to live in a subdivision with an HOA (homeowner's association) that might tell us that my husband's old pickup wasn't allowed in our own driveway or that we had to seek approval for paint colors on our home. We also didn't want to spend more of our money on a bigger house payment or devote more of our free time to maintaining a larger home.

But space was becoming a problem. Dale began to accumulate a lot of tools of his trade. I had a doll collection that took up a whole wall in our living room, and every closet was stuffed full of clothes. We never seemed to get rid of anything.

While our life at home was full of stuff, our love for the outdoors continued to grow. Instead of buying a larger home, in 1996 we bought a fishing boat. Coincidentally, the boat was also a 1979 model—our lucky year—in great condition. We began spending many of our weekends camping with friends at a small lake near Topeka or taking the boat to our local county park. We had long been outdoor people, and some of our most memorable dates as teenagers were spent at that county lake fishing, picnicking, and hiking the trails.

During this time, I also realized my dream of becoming a writer. My job at the credit facility was eliminated in 1998. I had worked there 10 years to the day, and my sever-ance package allowed me the freedom to start a freelance writing business. I began writing for small local newspapers and periodicals, building my way to a steady stringer job for a neighborhood division of *The Kansas City Star*. It wasn't my dream job at *Rolling Stone*, but after taking the long way to a career I was passionate about, it was good enough. Besides, working from home is great—I'm the best boss I've ever had.

## May–August 2003

When Mom sold the Wilson House in 1984, she (wisely) used most of the proceeds to pay off credit-card and loan debt. With the remainder, she entered into a venture with her brother and sister-in-law (my uncle Bud and aunt Kathy) to buy 30 acres of land in the Ozark Mountains.

Mom had been a housewife throughout her married life, until she opened the craft business, which she closed when she sold the Wilson House. After getting her own apartment, she began working as a clerk in a drugstore. She eventually realized she would most likely never have the money to build another home using the railroad pen-sion that she eventually aged into, so sometime in the early 1990s, she sold her 20 acres to my aunt Kathy, who had remarried after the death of my uncle.

In 1996, Mom was laid off from her retail job, and she moved from her two-bedroom apartment to a three-bedroom duplex a block from our house. Not only did the extra space mean that she could rescue some of her possessions from storage, but also her garage gave us extra space to store our boat and stuff that was now overflowing from our own home and shed.

That same year, Aunt Kathy and her new husband, Monty, began planning to build their dream home on the Ozarks land. They invited us down to camp and fish on beau-tiful Bull Shoals Lake, which the land abutted. We spent a few weekends a year there, helping them build their first cabin. They finally were able to retire to their dream home in 1999.

By 2002, Dale and I were visiting them regularly, enjoying the lake and woods that surrounded their home. At the end of the year, my aunt surprised us by gifting a small parcel of the land to us, provided that we build a home on it and not sell it.

We were ecstatic. We had always wanted a lake home of our own, where we could spend weekends and where we would eventually retire. We prepared to break ground on the 2.49 acres in the spring of 2003.

By the time we were planning on building Our Little Lake House, Mom's health was failing, and we knew she could not remain in the duplex for much longer. When we drew up the design for our house, we included plans for a 20-by-30-foot garage to store our boat and other *stuff* that had overflowed to her garage.

Aunt Kathy had construction experience and helped us create two designs using a computer-based architectural program. Financing was tight, but because we had never upsized in the city and our house payment there remained comfortable, we felt we could still swing another relatively small house payment.

The first home we designed was about 800 square feet, with a full basement and two bedrooms. However, we realized that we would need to go smaller in order to make the payments comfortable, so we opted for a 480-square foot one-bedroom design, thinking we could build a larger 1,000-square foot home after we moved there full-time. We would then use the smaller house as a guest cabin and my office.

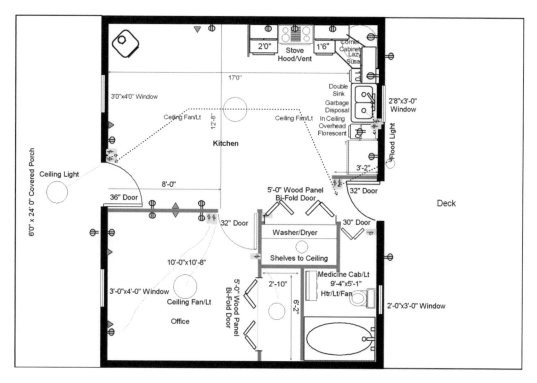

The final floor plans for Our Little House, with 480 square feet of interior living space, a covered front porch, and a back deck.

In the meantime, I knew I wanted a full kitchen (minus the dishwasher), a full bath with a tub, and room for a washer and dryer. We built a deep closet in the bedroom, complete with a hanging rod and shelves. The house was small enough that we skipped the expense of central air. Instead, we installed a window air-conditioner unit and planned to heat the home with a woodstove.

Our rural, unincorporated area didn't have a lot of building codes or ordinances, or a minimum-square-footage requirement as there are in some cities and towns. We did have to have some sort of water hookup and a permanent sewage system. In the country, that means a septic system. Our contractor had to hire an engineer to "perc" the property, which tests the soil to see how long it takes to drain. The septic tank has underground hoses with holes that allow the broken-down waste to run out into a leach field. If the soil doesn't drain properly, the system could eventually back up into a home.

We chose to avoid the major expense of digging a well and instead installed a 2,000-gallon water tank. A local water company delivered water when we needed it, which was suitable for washing clothes and bathing. We also skipped the expense of installing propane and installed only electric appliances. We saved money by not digging a full basement. Most of the mountains here are rock, so many homes only have a crawl space.

There were only two other permit requirements: We needed to make sure our house number was posted on our mailbox and gate, which makes it easier for first responders. And an occupancy permit was needed, which meant our contractor had to have a county building inspector look over the house when it was done to ensure it was a safe dwelling.

Construction underway in 2003 on Our Little Lake House.

We broke ground in May 2003, and Our Little House was finished by August. Although it was a five-hour drive from Kansas City, for the next three years, we spent every other weekend, plus holidays and vacations, at Our Little Lake House.

By the time the house was finished, Dale was a night supervisor in the diesel shop at the landfill. He would get off work around 3:30 Saturday mornings. On alternating weekends, as soon as he would get home, we'd load up our three dogs, and I would drive while Dale slept. I kept myself company with music. One of the songs I played a lot was "Tiny Dancer" by Elton John. In the classic hit, he sings of a tiny dancer counting the headlights on the highway.

I *felt* like I was dancing, driving through the early morning darkness, actually sometimes counting the headlights on our way to our tiny house in the woods. It was our escape to paradise. Even when I brought my writing work on vacations and long weekends, it didn't feel like I was actually working. By the time we'd arrive at Our Little Lake House around 10 a.m., we had most of the day left and all day on Sunday to play on the boat or have barbecues on the deck we dubbed the Party Deck for the good times we always have there. Since I was a freelance writer and Dale didn't have to be to work until 4 p.m. Monday, we typically stayed until Monday morning.

Our lives were going smoothly until my mom's health began to greatly deteriorate. By 2006, she became increasingly weak due to a major heart attack and end-stage chronic obstructive pulmonary disease (COPD), caused by nearly 60 years of smoking. She was no longer able to manage the stairs in her split-level duplex. Mom had almost always lived close to us. She didn't drive, so we did all of our grocery shopping and errands together. Now, Dale had to carry her in and out of her home so that we could take her to doctor's appointments.

I finally convinced her to move into a senior-living apartment building. She was using a walker by then, but she still wanted to maintain her independence. The building had no stairs, and it was close enough to our split-level that I could take her meals and check on her every day.

Still, moving to a smaller apartment meant she had to give up many of her things or put them in storage again, a prospect she found depressing.

When we were moving Mom, my nephew Shawn, who had lived with us for those three years after my dad died, noticed that the Wilson House was for sale. I asked him not to tell Mom. She missed the house so much that she never wanted to drive by it. She was already depressed at the prospect of moving into a senior apartment building. I knew the news would only make her more melancholy that she couldn't spend the rest of her days in her beloved Wilson House.

In the final six weeks of her life that winter of 2007, Mom was in the hospital more often than not. They determined she had contracted MRSA, an antibiotic-resistant infection that the public knew little about at the time. As a result of the MRSA, she contracted bacterial pneumonia. Only one drug was known to treat MRSA, and it had to be administered by IV in the hospital.

We had talked about moving full time later that year to Our Little Lake House. The landfill where Dale had worked for twenty-three years was selling, and we were relatively sure his job would be eliminated. I also somehow thought that if we all moved to the land, it would help fulfill Mom's dream of having her own home again, since the land had been purchased with money from the Wilson House.

For six weeks that winter, I sat by her bedside, urging her to fight so we could all move to that dream in the Ozark Mountains. But in that last week, my head told me she wasn't going to make it, although my heart never wanted to admit it.

She died on February 23.

I was heartbroken that I could not take my mom to show her our dream, the one initiated from the loss of her own, to show her that her dream was living on through ours.

The next three months were spent clearing out stuff—from my mom's apartment and our house. My aunt and I held a sale at her senior-living building, took what we wanted, distributed items according to her will, and put the rest in a storage facility.

I was more determined than ever to move. It had long been our dream to move to Our Little Lake House, where we could live in the woods and be on the lake full-time. Also, driving through our hometown everyday just reminded me of the route of the funeral procession. It was so painful for me that I cried almost every time I had to leave the house and drive that way. Our family and most of our friends were no longer in Turner, and the memories of the little burb I had once found so comforting were torture. I needed the comfort of Our Little Lake House, where I could always find peace. I needed to move forward and plan our future, which I pictured as much happier than our present.

## May 2007

Once we settled all of Mom's business, we began to prepare our split-level for sale. I knew that the first thing we had to do was deal with our 17 years of accumulated stuff. Ripping up old carpet and flooring, and painting was a piece of cake compared to clearing out the clutter. Stuff and more stuff was in every nook and cranny of the house, closets, garage, and shed.

We took truckloads for donation, and what wasn't worth saving went to the landfill. After renting another storage unit and staging the split-level according to instructions from our real estate agent, we finally put our house in the city on the market in May 2007. We received an offer within days.

Things were moving quickly. We had to be out of our split-level on June 30, the day before we boarded a plane for a 10-day trip to attend our German exchange daughter's wedding in Munich. We had been so focused on ridding our lives of clutter that we hadn't properly dealt with the grief of losing my mother, or for that matter, dealt with the fact that we were making several huge life changes, including moving out of our hometown and my husband leaving his job of 23 years.

Perhaps it was being in a foreign country so far from home, or perhaps it was the fact that we finally had time to exhale, but the events of the previous few months hit us hard one night while lying in bed in an apartment in Munich.

"I feel so lost without my mom, and I'm afraid for the future. What if we haven't done the right thing?" I asked Dale, tears starting to stream down my face. He turned and held me. At that moment, our only home was 300 miles from Kansas City, where Dale still held a job and where most of the people we knew still lived.

We were hit with new grief when we received word that night that one of our senior cats, Cali, had escaped the covered front porch, where we had blocked them in with gates until we got home and could deal with having them in closer quarters with the dogs. The pet sitter didn't find her before my aunt's dog did, and we would never see our Cali Cat again.

"I know," Dale said, still holding me. "I feel lost too." I think we both cried before we slept that night.

After we returned from Germany, we tried to sort through everything we had brought to Our Little Lake House. Although we had gotten rid of so much stuff, we still had enough to fill a large storage unit (which meant we had two, as we were still maintaining my mom's). Hauling our belongings to Our Little Lake House required a moving truck, a pickup, two trailers, and a small SUV.

Most of the stuff we took went into the garage that we built next to the house. We still planned on building a larger home, about 1,000 square feet, and using Our Little Lake House as my office and a guesthouse, but that was a dream in the making.

After the split-level sold, we settled our remaining bills in the city and spent a large chunk of money digging a permanent water well. Having the water tank had been fine for short visits, but the cost of having water delivered regularly was economically unsustainable. Whether we built the new house or not, we would still need a permanent water source. Well companies charge by the foot, and based on what neighbors told us they had paid for their wells, we estimated we would spend between $7,000 and $10,000. I woke up every day to the sound of the drill going deeper and deeper into the ground. Our well was so deep that we ended up having to put in casing to protect the pipe, and it cost us closer to $15,000.

After the move, Dale stayed with his sister in Kansas City while training the man who would take his job. (Although the job would be eliminated within the year, they had hired someone to replace Dale for the time being.) He was also actively applying online for jobs in our newly adopted town. He would drive down on Friday nights after work and stay until late Sunday night. He drove at night back to Kansas City to escape the heat of the day. It was exhausting for him and lonely for me, as I did not know anyone but Aunt Kathy and Monty.

Thankfully, it took Dale only three months after we returned from Munich to secure a job as a mechanic with a large boat-manufacturing plant near Our Little Lake House. It was time to obtain several bids to build the new larger home. However, we were shocked to find that construction costs had skyrocketed since building Our Little Lake House just four years earlier. After careful calculations, we realized we wouldn't be able to construct another house and maintain a level of comfort in our budget. I thought of my parents and how they had overextended later in life.

"There has to be a way," I told my Aunt Kathy. "I can't live in this tiny house." She agreed, as she had thought the 480-square-foot design was too small, even for weekend visits. We then obtained several bids for constructing an addition. Builders explained that we couldn't add on to the back of the house due to the roofline. It came in too low, and it would have been evident that the addition was an afterthought. Adding on to the side of the house that faced the sloping mountain was a possibility but was the most expensive option, as it would require a lot of fill and pouring a full basement. Additionally, the layout would be awkward; guests would have had to walk through our bedroom to get to the living room. Extending the front as far out as the covered porch would give us a few extra feet in the living room and bedroom, but would also eliminate the porch, one of my favorite spots.

As fall turned to winter, we decided to put any future building plans on hold until spring.

That winter passed, and we were cramped, especially since our 10-by-10-foot bedroom—which was smaller than the shed we had at the split-level—was doubling as my office. But we also found it very comfortable. The lower utility costs were wonderful; the lower mortgage payments made our budget even more manageable; and I could clean the house top to bottom in about an hour.

We realized that we loved the coziness of living in our small abode, and I loved the ease of maintaining it, which gave us more time to focus on new adventures. The money we were saving allowed us to travel back to Kansas City to visit friends and relatives several times during that first year. We also explored the parks around our new home. We were together more and tried new things, like bowling. (I had been on leagues when I was younger, but Dale still beat me every time!)

In the spring of 2008, we finally decided to leave Our Little Lake House as it was. Instead of expanding, we planned to build a separate office space—which we dubbed the Belle Writer's Studio in honor of my mother's middle name—and another garage for our boat and belongings that we had in storage in Kansas City. Dale was supportive of the plan as long as he had his garage space; he already got to boast that the garage we originally built in 2003 was bigger than our house. I was happy because I would have a dedicated office space.

We hadn't quite grasped the meaning of true downsizing and letting go of the unnecessary, but our accidental step into the tiny house movement had begun. Our Little Lake House became Our Little House.

# 2

# Living Large Is the American Dream:
## A History of Square Footage
## in the United States

*Living Truth:* *"I have spent my life judging the distance between
American reality and the American dream."*
**—Bruce Springsteen**

What is the American Dream? According to Investopedia.com, a leading finance website, "The American dream offers the freedom to make both the large and small decisions that affect one's life; the freedom to aspire to bigger and better things and the possibility of achieving them; the freedom to accumulate wealth; the opportunity to lead a dignified life; and the freedom to live in accordance with one's values, even if those values are not widely held or accepted."[1]

Since Colonial times, the American Dream has included homeownership—owning a piece of property that is all yours and cannot be easily taken away and is not subject to the whims of landlords. However, the focus of the dream has changed over the years from what we *need* to what we *want*.

At the beginning of the twentieth century, my paternal grandparents lived in a two-bedroom cabin with a dirt floor while raising thirteen children. My grandfather was a coal miner and farmer, and my grandmother took care of the house and raised the children.

My paternal grandfather, Frank Fivecoat, Sr., at age 73 (top left); my paternal grandmother, Nora Lee Hixon Fivecoat in 1952 (top right); my maternal grandparents, Francis and Mildred Wagner with their two children, my mother Betty and her brother Francis (bottom left); my parents, Betty Wagner and Frank Fivecoat, just before their wedding in April 1945 (bottom right).

My maternal grandparents, my mom, and my uncle lived in a small flat in a German Lutheran neighborhood in the area known as the Back of the Yards on the South Side of Chicago, where my grandfather worked as an early union organizer in the meat industry. My grandfather died suddenly of cancer at age 28, at which point my grandmother moved the family to her parents' farm in Missouri, where other extended family members also lived. As children, both my parents not only shared a bedroom, but often shared a bed with siblings or cousins. For both of my sets of grandparents, the American Dream was built around providing their children with the basics of food and shelter. They did not have material wealth, but they lived dignified lives in accordance with their values. My mom often spoke of the hardships of living with so many family members on her grandfather's farm during the Great Depression. But even though they may have received only an orange, a piece of candy, and a small toy in their stockings for Christmas, she always insisted it was the happiest time of her life.

♠

That American Dream—to live simply and within one's means—changed for Depression Era people after World War II with the rise of the modern American middle class. In 1950, just a couple of years after my parents bought their bungalow, which was originally about 600 square feet, the average size of new American homes was 983 square feet. An upward trend continued throughout the twentieth century. According to census data, the average new-built American home in 1973 measured 1,525 square feet. By 2007, that number had swollen to 2,277.[2] As square footage increased, family size decreased. In 1973, the average number of people per household in the United States was 3.01; in 2007, it was 2.56.[3]

Why were Americans, who were having smaller families, building bigger homes? As American wages began to rise, so did the middle class. The median household income in 1973 was $8,983, compared to $48,117 in 2007. Adjusted for inflation, this would be $48,557 in 1973, compared to $55,627 in 2007.[4] Americans began to see their homes not just as a place to shelter their family, but also as an investment for their wealth portfolio. And it wasn't just homes—families had to have cars to fill those one- and two- and (finally) three-car garages. They also wanted more stuff to fill their bigger and bigger homes. "Keeping up with the Joneses" became as American as apple pie and baseball.

That all changed in 2008 with the arrival of the Great Recession. Some economists partly blame the near global economic collapse on an unsustainable housing bubble that finally burst. Too much mortgage debt carried by too many people in developed nations and the subprime lending crisis in the United States allowed borrowers to take loans on houses they couldn't actually afford.

When the economy nearly failed, demand decreased for the ever-growing Mc-Mansion, and the American housing market started to see a slight decline in average square footage for new homes. The average square footage went from 2,571 in 2007 to 2,519 in 2008. It continued to decline in 2009, to 2,438.[5] Median household income also decreased slightly during the Great Recession from $48,117 in 2007 to $47,690 in 2009. Confidence in the American Dream was shaken to its core.

## History of the Tiny House Movement

Prior to the recession, there was a small and relatively quiet movement afoot. The tiny house movement at that time consisted mostly of people who wanted to downsize not so much for financial reasons, but to leave a smaller footprint on the environment and to lead simpler lives.

People in the movement had discovered that the American Dream wasn't about buying bigger homes and accumulating more stuff. It was about *living* (not just *having*) and doing what's important with those you love. These pioneers could be described as hippies, or modern homesteaders who loved nature and the outdoors. They left cities and suburbs, which have strict code restrictions, and built homes in rural areas that had no square-footage minimums. Some built homes totally off grid, using solar panels, composting toilets, and rainwater collection systems. These modern homesteaders spent their free time hiking, fishing, and doing whatever else they enjoyed. They discovered that *Living Large is a state of mind*, which I think should be the true motto of the movement.

The tiny house movement isn't a rigid organization with a leadership structure, activists, or lobbyists. It's a group of people all over the world who have discovered that living in a small or tiny home can free them of the financial burden of a large mortgage, allowing them more time and freedom to explore their passions. Additionally, it can lessen their footprint on the environment.

The "movement" moniker originated in print and online media. Awareness grew as the public was exposed to blogs and social media pages dedicated to little house living. When new reality shows on the tiny house life hit cable television, interest exploded. The new FYI channel (formerly Bio) launched *Tiny House Nation* in the summer of

2014. The series focuses on contractors who help people build their new tiny homes and get rid of their stuff to downsize to tiny house life. It also provides photo examples of other small and tiny houses. HGTV recently launched three new shows: *Tiny House Hunters*; *Tiny House, Big Living*; and *Tiny House Builders*.

The movement has no leaders, but there are pioneers. For example, Lloyd Kahn, founder of Shelter Publications, has been writing books about build-it-yourself tiny homes for years. Sarah Susanka is also the author of books about making the most of the space you have. Jay Shafer, founder of Tumbleweed Tiny House Company and Four Lights Tiny House Company, which design and build tiny homes, and Gregory Johnson, who co-founded the Small House Society, are two others who have been involved in the direction of the movement.

While some folks may have been living in small or tiny homes for years without realizing they were a part of broader movement, hundreds of thousands of people worldwide have realized they are part of something special. Others are armchair enthusiasts who dream about "someday."

Kent Griswold was one of those armchair enthusiasts. The 57-year-old lives in Bend, Oregon. He loved the idea of little and tiny homes, and in 2007, when he discovered there was actually a small movement starting to gain traction, he decided to blog about it. He was surprised when TinyHouseBlog.com almost immediately began receiving over 10,000 hits per day. As word spread about this "new" lifestyle, other blogs began popping up.

When we moved full-time into Our Little House in 2007, I had no idea there was a movement. After living there for two years, I began to take note of the many ways in which our lives had changed and thought it would make a great topic to write about. I had managed several blogs, and the idea for LivingLargeinOurLittleHouse.com was born. After I started blogging, I connected with Kent, who told me all about this tiny house phenomenon.

By that time, the house of cards had begun to crumble for many homeowners who had overextended themselves by purchasing houses they couldn't afford. According to RealtyTrac, a real estate data company, 2.8 million homeowners received notice of foreclosure in 2009. That was up by 21 percent from the previous year and up a whopping 120 percent from 2007.[6] Out of necessity, people began to explore the possibility of actually living within their means and owning only what they need.

From data I've gathered from my readers, interest in the tiny house movement spans all generations. In the aftermath of the recession, younger Baby Boomers (born between 1955 and 1964) and Gen Xers (born between 1964 and 1981) began to realize that working just to pay a mortgage was a waste. These tiny house pioneers sought a simpler lifestyle that allowed them to follow their passions, like owning a home-based business, traveling the country or world, or spending more time with family or outdoors. Whatever their passions, people were making the decision to downsize so that they could work to live, not live to work.

The Millennials (those born between 1980 and 2000) appear to have more practical ideas. Burdened with large student loans and faced with brutally high rents in large cities, these young adults began to seek out ways they could afford to live.

And as older Baby Boomers (born between 1946 and 1954) enter retirement (according to the Pew Research Center, each day approximately 10,000 Americans turn 65[7]), they too are feeling the urge to simplify their lives. Many Boomers no longer need or want the burden of caring for the larger homes in which they raised their families.

How is the movement defined as "tiny" vs. "small"? There is some disagreement within the movement on what defines a "tiny" house and what defines a "small" (or "little") house. Some describe "tiny" as less than 300 square feet; others define "tiny" as less than 400 square feet and "small" as less than 500 square feet.

I generally refer to a "small" (or "little") house as having under 1,200 square feet. (And in this book, I use the terms "tiny house," "small house," and "little house" interchangeably.) But to me, Living Large is more about a state of mind and less about square footage. For example, a family of four moving from a 4,000-square-foot space to 1,200 square feet might feel that they are living in a tiny space. It depends on what each family *needs*—without wasting space, managing excessive stuff, and/or spending too much time on maintenance. If the family were to be unhappy in anything less, it really wouldn't be living well.

## The Tiny House Movement Today

The average-size new home in America was on the rise in 2013, reaching an all-time high of 2,646 square feet.[8] The data show that the average size of a new home dropped again in 2014, to 2,453 square feet, which may be, in part, a result of the rise of the little house movement.[9]

Additionally, overall homeownership is on the decline, and some people who are not buying traditional homes are building or buying tiny homes. According to a 2014 census report, homeownership was at its peak in 2004, with 69.2 percent of Americans in their own homes. In the first quarter of 2014, that number dropped to 64.8 percent, the lowest it's been since 1995. By third quarter 2014, the rate dropped to 64.4 percent and fell again in the first quarter 2015 to 63.7 percent.[10]

"The homeownership rate is held back by slow job growth, tight mortgage credit and declining affordability," Jed Kolko, then chief economist of Trulia Inc., told Bloomberg Business in an interview in April 2014. "We'll see it stay around this level for some time."[11] Slow job growth, tight mortgage credit, and declining affordability are all factors that draw enthusiasts to the small house movement and away from traditional homeownership.

Recent polls suggest that traditional homeownership may no longer be the gold standard of the American Dream. In 2013, Credit.com conducted a study of Americans 18 to 24 years old and found that 27.9 percent defined the American Dream as being able to retire by age 65; 23 percent defined it as being debt-free, and only 18.2 percent defined the American Dream as owning a home.[12]

Still, people need to hang their hat somewhere, and unlike in decades past when it was usually cheaper to rent than to buy, rental rates have also skyrocketed. This is another reason that the tiny house movement has become increasingly attractive.

## Codes: The New Frontier of the Movement

Data aren't readily available on how many people are living in tiny homes in the United States. Homeownership data are typically collected by the mortgage industry, and since real estate experts say 68 percent of tiny home dwellers don't have a mortgage,[13] data are difficult to find. However, the National Association of REALTORS estimates that little homes under 1,000 square feet make up about 1 percent of the market.[14]

If so many people are interested in the idea of little house living, why aren't there more folks living that dream? A primary factor is that many people don't believe they can give up their large homes (and all their stuff) and still be happy. Dale and I didn't think we could, until we did. But the movement is also held back in part due to building codes on minimum square footage, and requirements for permanent water, sewer, and electrical sources.

The majority of people building or buying little homes are building or parking them in rural areas because codes in most cities don't allow for tiny homes. In addition, cities generally require dwellings to have a permanent water source and flushing toilets (while many portable tiny homes have composting toilets).

Many of these codes were put into place after the Great Depression and during the post–World War II boom. During the Depression, people were forced to create shanty-towns just to have a place to sleep. Most of these dwellings were not only unsightly, but also unsafe. Local governments wanted to make sure residents were building safe homes and not "tenements" or "shantytowns."

In addition, many counties, cities and states haven't figured out how to define a tiny home on wheels. Many people build mobile tiny homes so they can travel and take their home with them. Tiny homes on wheels are generally better insulated and built to last longer than a traditional recreational vehicle. Moreover, they're designed for full time living, while a recreational vehicle is not. But cities and counties don't know how to classify a tiny home on wheels. Is it a mobile home? An RV or a guest structure, particularly when it is parked in someone's driveway or backyard? Each local jurisdiction has its own ordinances, and the definitions vary. Therefore, some people living in tiny homes may be doing so outside of the law, putting themselves at risk of fines or even losing their homes.

People who want this lifestyle must pick up the torch and take it to the next step.

One of these cases involves Michael Brown and his wife, Ann. In a highly publicized 2015 case in Chesterfield, Virginia, the Browns sought to live the tiny house dream in a home built on an 8½-by-20-foot trailer. The cute little home featured beige siding, a red door, and even a little white picket fence on the front porch. Aside from the wheels underneath, it looked just like a miniature suburban home. They parked it in the back-yard of their large property and rented out the main house.

According to the local ABC News affiliate, the home was classified by the county as a recreational vehicle, and local codes prevented people from living in those types of dwellings full-time. "Both the building code and the zoning ordinances probably have some catching up to do," Ron Clements, Chesterfield Building Inspection Assistant Director, told ABC.[15]

In one town in Arkansas, the city council voted in the spring of 2015 to ban homes under 600 square feet from the town. The local ABC affiliate there reported, "They believe banning tiny houses, homes smaller than 600 square feet, will also improve the landscape and beautify the residential area around Walnut Ridge."[16] It appears that the council has the NIMBY attitude (Not in My Backyard) and still believes the tiny house movement is akin to the shantytowns of the last century.

There have been some victories, however, in changing the codes and ordinances around the country. Portland, Oregon, long a hub for the tiny house movement, has some of the most relaxed laws in the country. Cities and towns such as St. Cloud (Minnesota), Madison (Wisconsin), and Spur (Texas) have redefined their minimum-square-footage requirements for new and remodeling construction, embracing the movement.

In other areas, some RV parks are beginning to advertise as "tiny house friendly." One such place is Orlando Lakefront at College Park, which advertises on its website that it is one of the first RV parks in the country to solve the challenge of where to park a tiny home.

Several nonprofits and organizations that assist the poor have also been helping homeless people get into tiny homes, and they've been successful in establishing code-compliant communities. Occupy Madison, a nonprofit in Wisconsin, raised money and built three homes on private property. In November 2014, the first occupants moved in just prior to the cold setting in. The nonprofit plans to add an additional four homes to the community, as well as a community center, as soon as funds are raised through donations.[17]

One of the tiny homes built by Occupy Madison.

Operation Northern Comfort and A Tiny Home for Good, two nonprofit organizations that help the homeless in Syracuse (New York), are hoping to build three tiny homes on a vacant lot on that city's south side. According to news reports, the lot is owned by the county.[18] The nonprofits are hoping to buy it so they can build the tiny homes using donations and proceeds from fund-raisers. Residents would be selected based on an application process and would pay rent based on income. The nonprofits hope the effort is just the beginning of helping end homelessness in the city through building tiny homes.

In another highly publicized 2015 story, the town of Waveland (Mississippi) decided to allow tiny homes under 574 square feet to be built in order to ease a housing shortage that resulted from Hurricane Katrina. Pye Parson and her son lost their home in Waveland during the hurricane and moved to Birmingham, Alabama. Pye, a realtor, dreamed of returning to Waveland with her new husband. The television show *Tiny House Nation* highlighted that dream in an episode documenting their 500-square-foot home being built.

However, prior to production, they had to clear a zoning ordinance that required the frontage of homes to be half of the size of the lot, which in the Parsons' case, would have resulted in a house with at least 1,200 square feet.

Once the variance was given on the zoning, the tiny white home was built. It sits on stilts (as many do near the ocean) and features 12'-to-19'-high ceilings, both of which make the house appear much larger. The home includes two bedrooms and plenty of outdoor living space.

Mayor Mike Smith said on the show that he was convinced that little homes may be the way to help his community continue to rebuild. News reports have since suggested the mayor is looking into working with a developer to build a tiny house community.[19]

If you want to build a tiny home in someone's backyard, many local ordinances, especially those in cities with a high retiree population, allow for "mother-in-law" quarters on the property of larger homes (now referred to as accessory dwelling units). These typically cannot be on wheels, however, and must have power, water, and sewer hookups on a separate utility or connected to the main house.

Whether it is in a city or a rural area, never embark on building a little home without first thoroughly checking out the local county, city and/or state regulations regarding building codes. It's also a good idea to first consult with a local builder with experience constructing little homes, as he or she may be knowledgeable about local building codes/laws. Foregoing these steps could turn your dream home into a nightmare.

Insurance is another major issue to be aware of when you have a tiny house on wheels. Even if your home is debt-free, you may still want to get insurance for fire or for the loss of items inside your home. Many companies that build tiny homes on wheels can refer you to insurance companies, since their homes are in the same classification as mobile or prefab homes or RVs. In addition, see the Resources section in this book for agencies that may be able to help you insure your tiny home. Luckily, since Our Little

House and the Belle Writer's Studio are on permanent foundations, we didn't have any issues obtaining insurance through a major insurer.

When the codes and insurance frontiers are conquered, I predict that the tiny house movement will become a more accepted way of life in America and around the world. People will begin to recognize that living in a small space allows each person to achieve the definition of the American Dream that includes "the freedom to make both the large and small decisions that affect one's life; the freedom to aspire to bigger and better things and the possibility of achieving them; the freedom to accumulate wealth and the opportunity to lead a dignified life; and the freedom to live in accordance with one's values."

# 3

# The Definition of a Little House
# Is What You Need:
## Finding the Right Size and Place
## for Your Family

*Living Truth: It's not how big the house is, but how happy the home is.*

I heard the *kerplunk!* I just didn't realize it was me until something furry started wiggling its way out from beneath me and my foot started throbbing. Dale had a history of falling out of bed—he had broken his collarbone doing it as a toddler. When he fell out of bed as an adult, he didn't usually hurt himself, so it was typically me stifling a giggle and asking, "Are you okay?" This time it was me doing the falling, and I landed on Emma, our German shepherd/rottweiler mix, thankfully not hurting her. Dale woke up for a moment and when he realized I had fallen, he was the one who got the laugh that night. I was wedged in the cramped space between our bed and my mother's antique dresser. The throbbing in my left ankle told me I was going to have one heck of a bruise.

When Dale and I rented our first duplex, our first major purchase was a king-size water bed set, popular in the mid-'80s. It completely overwhelmed the largest bedroom in our duplex. When we purchased the split-level, we'd had enough of leaking mattresses and decided a queen-size bed would be big enough.

It was, until we allowed up to three dachshunds to sleep in the bed too. In Our Little

House, the bed I fell out of that morning was full size. We had two large dogs, Emma and Sade, plus two dachshunds still in the bed, and I hadn't quite gotten used to the loss of those few inches. After twisting and turning to get back into bed, I spent the rest of the night wishing we had a little more space.

Getting up from the sofa for a bowl of popcorn (or, if we're being really naughty, a bowl of ice cream) is much like the old game of Twister, where you put your feet and hands on different circles and get tangled up with other players. Only when we get up, we have to step over paws, dog beds, furry heads, and wagging tails. Put a foot in the wrong spot, and we lose the game. It suits us and we make it work, but a few feet more would make a big difference.

When we originally designed Our Little Lake House to be a weekend and vacation home, my aunt and my mom told us to build as much as we felt we could afford. They advised that we might never have the opportunity to build that other larger house we had planned on when we moved out of the city.

As it turned out, they were right. We could have built the larger home I had dreamed of—the one with a dining area large enough for our dining table, a kitchen with a break-fast bar, a living room with a cathedral ceiling and tall rock fireplace, and a bedroom large enough for a queen-size bed, and a master bath with a walk-in shower and separate tub. You get the idea. We *could* have had that larger home, but we would have been strapped with debt and an uncomfortably hefty mortgage payment.

It was more important for me to live out my life passions, one of which is my dogs. When we moved to Our Little House, I wanted to adopt rescue dogs, as many as we could afford. I have had dogs all of my life, beginning with a shepherd/collie mix named Smokey. My parents made her stay outside (or in the basement on very cold nights), and that never felt right to me. Smokey accompanied me on bike rides, walked with me to the store, and was my protector if any neighborhood bully threatened me. I vowed that when I grew up, I wouldn't have "outside dogs," but dogs that were treated as full members of the family.

In that summer of 2007, when we moved full-time into Our Little House, we had three dogs: Molly, a red dapple dachshund; Dakota, a black dachshund/beagle mix; and Emma, our German shepherd/rottweiler mix. We also had our two senior cats, 15-year-old Cali and 18-year-old Tabitha. All were rescues, or what I like to call "recycled" pets—animals no one else wanted but who fit into our family perfectly.

Our family grew by one more on a hot summer evening, the night before our big move. We saw a black-and-white dog being led by a leash next to a car on the side of the road in Kansas City, Kansas, off of a highway.

Our two senior cats, Tabitha (left) and Cali (right).

I figured they were traveling and had stopped to let their dog do its business. Several seconds later, I looked in my rearview mirror and saw that the car was now behind me, and behind it, trying valiantly to catch up, was the dog.

"Those assholes just dumped that poor dog! Look, it's chasing those people trying to catch them!" I slowed down, and the car sped past. I looked in the mirror again and saw the dog heading into the ditch alongside the road. I drove for a couple of more minutes, my eyes blurry with tears, trying to get the dog out of my head. I knew it wouldn't last long on that road without being hit by a car. I whipped the truck into the next side road and turned around.

"The only thing that surprised me was how long it took you to turn around," Dale said at the time.

Sade made four dogs moving into Our Little House. Those beginning days weren't easy. We learned that Sade had a strong prey drive. So when we headed to Germany for our exchange daughter's wedding immediately following our move, we tried to confine the cats temporarily to the covered front porch. The cats had ventured outside when we lived in the city, but usually never went farther than the deck. At Our Little House we had no reason to believe they would try so hard to break through the blocks we had set up on the covered front porch and escape to the yard, but they were in an unfamiliar place with someone they didn't know taking care of them. We learned of Cali's death while still in Germany and leaving them out there while we were gone is a mistake I will regret for the rest of my life.

Having your pets in a tiny home is very doable with a little planning. If I had known about catteries (huge wire enclosures designed to keep cats confined to porches or decks) then, we would have gotten one for the covered front porch to protect them better and figured out a more permanent solution when we returned from overseas.

Some of our dogs in and around the house (clockwise from top left): Abbi, Dakota (Boo), Chloe, and Dexter.

Trying to keep the cats separate from Sade is the only time we felt as if our space wasn't right for our family. Tabitha died shortly after we returned from Germany; she was 18 and suffered kidney failure, most likely from the stress of the move. We have had up to seven dogs in the house at any given time—some permanent and some fosters while we found them a forever home.

Shortly before we lost Emma in the summer of 2010, we rescued Chloe, a black lab mix. Abbi, a husky/shepherd mix, joined our family from a high kill shelter that fall. About a year later, Dale brought home a skinny beagle mix we named Dexter. Before we lost Molly to old age in 2013, we had six dogs full-time in 480 square feet. We may feel like we're learning new balancing moves as we step over dogs and dog beds, but except for the time I fell out of bed, I've never fallen in the house. I've tripped over my own feet in the driveway, but that's another story that may have won us a prize on *America's Funniest Home Videos* if anyone had been there to film it.

Our expense budget for dog care is now as full as our house, but Our Little House has always felt the right size for our family, no matter how many dogs I've added. I guess that's because they *are* our family, living beings that have taught us so much about caring and loving unconditionally. It wouldn't be Our Little House without them.

## It's All in the Details

When we married, we purchased so much of our furniture from the department store giant J.C. Penney that Dale jokingly called our split-level home "The J.C. Penney Showroom." One of my most prized pieces of furniture in that showroom is my china cabinet, which has a light that highlights some of my prettiest pieces of glassware at night, including pieces of china my beloved late great-aunt made for me.

It isn't a huge cabinet, but there isn't a good place for it in Our Little House. Since we weren't planning on making the house our full-time residence, I didn't design a place for it. While I don't *need* that cabinet, this lifestyle is about living with the people (and in our case, the pets) and things we love. There are just some things we can't or shouldn't pluck from our lives. That's okay, as long as we don't have so many things that they interfere with actual living.

I will talk more about what to do with heirlooms, handed-down items, and sentimental pieces in Chapter 12, but this is another reason we wish we had taken my mom and aunt's advice and built as if we weren't going to build another home.

One way to get your tiny living space just right is to practice before living it. You can do this by renting various small vacation cabins, which will give you an excellent idea of the size and style you want. We actually found a perfect cabin for us, albeit too late.

While we stayed in a couple of cabins before our build, I wish we had stayed in more to get additional ideas. A few years after moving to Our Little House, we stayed at the Oak Haven Resort and Spa, a community that has different-size cabins in the Great Smoky Mountains in Sevierville, Tennessee. We were in a one-bedroom, 600-square-foot cabin that featured cathedral ceilings, which always makes a place feel more spacious. Its open design, with a combination living room and kitchen, had enough space for a full-size sofa and chair, a breakfast bar, and a kitchen table.

The bedroom with adjoining bath was also spacious, with a king-size bed, large sunken tub, and separate luxury shower.

"This is perfect," I told Dale upon arrival. He smiled and said, "Let's just go back and get the dogs and live here." Only then did we realize how important it is, when designing a little home, to stay at as many different vacation rentals as possible. It not only allows a couple or family to get a feel for a small space, but also helps them decide what they need and what they can live without.

Jay Shafer, founder of the Tumbleweed Tiny Houses and now the owner of Four Lights Tiny House Company in Cotati, California, even suggests that people thinking of going small should camp in a tent. "You learn pretty quickly what you need," Jay said. "The first and hardest step is figuring out what one needs to be happy and getting rid of the rest."

While the cabin at Oak Haven gave us an idea of what would work better for us, the cabin floor plan, as with most vacation rentals, would have needed some modification for full-time use. It needed at least one additional closet and space for a washer/dryer, but it was everything we wished we had in Our Little House. And with the tall ceilings and copious outdoor deck and porch space, it was the perfect size. Outdoor living space is very important to tiny house living, as it provides access to the unlimited space of the outdoors, as well as space for entertaining.

To try out living in a smaller space, Misti McCloud, 43, and her partner, Steven Chrystal, 34, decided to rent a furnished 750-square-foot vacation cabin in the Pisgah National Forest, in the mountains of western North Carolina, for six months. Misti had a corporate career and lived in a spacious two-bedroom apartment with a master bedroom and walk-in closet in the D.C. suburbs when she decided to downsize her life and become a full-time freelance writer. After renting the cabin during one Memorial Day weekend, she and Steven decided to start her new life outside of the corporate world in the same cabin through the winter.

Misti McCloud and Steven Chrystal (inset) spent a winter in this 750-square-foot cabin nestled in the Pisgah National Forest in North Carolina.

The cabin was furnished, so Misti had to choose whether to store most of her possessions or get rid of them. She sold 90 percent of her things—even her flat-screen television—and put most of what was left in storage. "I only kept out a few items of clothing, my laptop, and some pillows," she says.

Living in the cabin—which has a bedroom loft large enough for a full-size bed and a dresser—has taught Misti a lot about what she'll be looking for in a permanent residence. "I definitely want to continue living in a small space so I can Live Large," Misti says. "But moving forward, I'll only live in one-level places. The cabin I'm in currently has a loft, and the older I get, the more difficult those stairs become."

Misti's experience highlights what is at the heart of the movement—not getting hung up on square footage, but finding a size and layout that's comfortable for you. Home is what feels right and fits your needs. *Living Large is a state of mind.*

This is the message Sarah Susanka has been promoting since the publication of her book, *The Not So Big House,* in 1998. Sarah first discovered tiny living when she downsized to a 96-square-foot home during college. The house had a woodstove, a bunk above the closet, a foldout desk, and an outhouse. "It was very simple," Sarah says. "I had to make a little go a long way. I loved the experience."

As Sarah was completing her formal education to become an architect, she married the idea of designing a home with her experience in that 96-square-foot space. "I began to understand that the quality of a home has almost nothing to do with size," she says. "If a home is tailored to the way we actually live and not to how we think we should live, and if it is beautiful and inspirational, it will make us happier."

For example, Sarah believes that many people do not need both a formal and casual dining area in their home. "It's all about designing an everyday space that can be transformed into that formal space we might need one or two times a year," she says.

Kevin Kalley and his partner, David Currier, both in their 60s, had this design concept in mind when they built their 480-square-foot home on the island of Hawaii in 2011. The house was initially a vacation home, but Kevin and David knew they would retire to their little home in the future. Some of the design elements they chose reflected this forethought, such as a Murphy bed in the living room that's hidden by sliding bamboo panels. The living room also features recessed shelving built into the wall that contains media equipment for the flat-screen television that hangs on the wall. The shelving is hidden by a piece of favorite artwork.

Kevin Kalley and his partner, David Currier (left), optimized space throughout their 480-square-foot home on the island of Hawaii (center), even purchasing a dining table with storage drawers (right).

Their kitchen is compact but fully equipped for two people who love to cook and entertain. Cabinets have pull-downs, slide-outs, and access to blind corners. A pot rack maximizes space for cooking gear. A foldout dining table the couple purchased from IKEA has shelves for storage underneath and can seat up to six guests. Pocket doors (which slide into the wall) throughout the home allow for privacy without taking up prime space. In addition, outdoor space is plentiful, and thanks to the lovely climate, Kevin and David often entertain on the lanai. Although their house is the same square footage as Our Little House, in the photos and videos I've seen it feels more open due to the layout and large windows and doors, which allow for more light.

♦

When designing a small space, making it sustainable for the long term is important. However, we can't always foretell the future. "Oopsie" babies happen, for example. But people don't *have* to upsize to a new home every time a bundle of joy comes along. Jane Mosher, who is now 69, moved into her 22-by-32-foot modular home in an eastern township of Quebec, Canada, in 1966. She raised three boys in that modest space. After her children were gone, she remodeled it to fit her empty-nest lifestyle. Jane comes from a generation that adapted homes to fit their families and lifestyles, which melds perfectly with the little home concept of making a home sustainable. We can usually, if we want, stay in our small space, just as Jane has for the past fifty years.

Rebecca (Bec) Peterson Gawtry, 31, and her husband, Doug, 33, lived together in a 1,200-square-foot home until they got married in 2007. After the wedding, they moved into a 728-square-foot home on a lake in Minnesota. A short time later, they learned that Rebecca was pregnant. But that wasn't the only big news. "Not long after that, we learned that we were having twins," Bec says. "Four people and a dog in 700 square feet? That seemed pretty crazy, but the bottom had fallen out of the real estate market, and selling the house wasn't an option."

Even if selling their little home had been an option, they'd fallen in love with their lakefront property. "We wanted to live in a recreational area, and when we were looking at houses, nothing bigger was available," says Bec. After the Gawtrys found out they were having twins of the same sex, they knew they could make it work. "We only wanted two kids, and it would be easier to stay in our two-bedroom because the girls could share a bedroom," says Bec.

Not long after they learned they were having twins, Bec and Doug bumped into the former owners of their little house at a local store. "She was also pregnant and always hated the house because it was so small," says Bec.

When Bec told the couple she was pregnant, the husband said, "Well, I guess you're going to have to move now." Bec and Doug indicated that they were staying in their little home. "The former owner said, 'You're going to raise a baby in that tiny house?' And I said, 'No, I'm going to raise *two* babies there!'"

Twins Evelyn and Nora have lived with their parents, Rebecca and Doug Gawtry, in a 728-square-foot little home their whole lives.

As the tiny house movement continued to evolve, Jay Shafer began to notice a need for younger couples to have the option to add space if they have children. Jay's personal tiny house journey began in 1997 when he began renovating the Airstream trailer that he lived in full-time.

Two years later, he built a 100-square-foot home that won a "Most Innovative Design" in *Natural Home Magazine*'s House of the Year Contest. Jay founded Tumbleweed Tiny Houses and sold his first house in 2003. "The media and people got pretty excited," Jay recalled. "The pendulum was just beginning to swing from McMansions, and the paradigm was starting to shift toward smaller."

By 2012, Jay was married and living in a 500-square-foot home with his wife and two sons. Jay says that rather than living in a rural area, as he did when he lived in his first tiny home, he feels that living in a smaller house than what most families live in near the center of town is a good fit for him. He resigned from Tumbleweed that year, "for more freedom and more manageability." He founded Four Lights and began focusing on how younger couples could buy or build a tiny home and also plan for future children.

Jay's own two sons were an inspiration for designing what he is calling the U-House, which stands for Universal House (not to be confused with Universal Design, which incorporates design elements for people with physical limitations). First, the U-House avoids some of the zoning issues that other tiny homes or trailers must contend with because it can be zoned as either a park-model RV, manufactured housing, modular, or site-built construction. The prefab construction starts with a 200-square-foot base with a sleeping loft. It is built to add an extra bedroom. Now a single dad living in a 112-square-foot tiny home again, Jay is designing a U-House of his own, where he and his boys will be comfortable.

The contractible and retractable space design for Jay's tiny homes allows people a budget-friendly way to add onto their space, should the need arise, without having the cost and maintenance of additional space if they don't need it.

🏠

New additions to the family aren't the only events that might change a household's needs. Tammy Strobel and her husband Logan Smith began dreaming about a tiny house in 2007, when they were both 28 years old. "We were living in Davis, California, which was insanely expensive," Tammy says. "We realized we could live in a tiny house and pay cash for it."

Saving for their house took a while, but in 2010, they hired Portland Alternative Dwellings (PAD)—the company owned by Dee Williams, author of *The Big Tiny*—to build their 128-square-foot tiny home. Once their dream was completed, they finally moved in 2011. Before building the home, Tammy realized they were onto something special, and she began documenting the couple's downsizing at rowdykittens.com.

Tammy and Logan's plan was to move their tiny home to Chico, California, to a lot previously occupied by a mobile home. The couple assumed their home would be parked legally on the property, since a mobile home had been acceptable. But after they moved and got settled, someone notified city officials, and they learned that their tiny home wasn't considered a mobile home and didn't adhere to code.

The home, which doesn't have a permanent water source and doesn't hook up to the sewer system (it has a composting toilet), didn't meet the city's standards for a structure in which people were living full-time. "They wanted to work with us, but to modify our tiny home would have cost around $30,000," says Tammy. "It was too much for us, and we just decided to move back to Northern California and park on Logan's parents' property, where it is legal."

Their tiny home was still sitting legally on family property when Tammy injured her back in 2013. She couldn't move without pain for a month, which also meant that she couldn't climb into the couple's bedroom loft. The window seat folds out into an extra bed, but it did make the couple think about the challenges of aging in their tiny home.

Tammy Strobel documents living in this tiny home with her husband and their two cats on rowdykittens.com.

Tammy had trouble climbing into the tiny bedroom loft (left) when she hurt her back, so she slept on the extra bed that folds out from the window seat (right).

After enduring the brutal winter of 2013–2014 and dealing with their water hose to the tiny house freezing, Tammy and Logan decided to rent a 700-square-foot cottage in Yreka, California, for the following winter. "Logan's grandparents are in their 90s, and they are too disabled to get into the tiny," Tammy says. "The cottage has two bedrooms, and my mom can come and visit now, and it doesn't feel as cramped."

Tammy and Logan have faced code issues, injury that prevented her from climbing into the loft, brutal winters, and how to handle visiting and aging relatives in their tiny home. They are now deciding what size house will suit them best, both now and for the long term. They are committed to living sustainably, but are not yet sure how small they are willing to go.

More mature couples who don't expect any more major life changes in the future still have to plan for their small house lifestyle. Connie and Ken Howe, both in their early

60s, have had long, successful careers. Although they could have afforded to stay in their 2,400-square-foot, four-bedroom, three-bath home with a three-car garage, they no longer wanted the large payments or maintenance required. "We reached the point in our lives when we realized that more stuff doesn't make you happy," says Connie. "We found ourselves camping in our trailer almost every weekend and found out we were more relaxed and happier in a small space."

They looked for a spot where they could build a little home and fell in love with Lost Lake Resort, just outside of Olympia, Washington. Lost Lake is an "air space condo park." Instead of traditional condominiums, which are typically adjoined in one building, an air space condo is an individual unit. The owners of the unit own the lot on which it sits, along with an undivided percentage of common areas.

In the Howes' park, owners buy lots and can either place a park model cabin or a larger RV on the property. They can landscape, put up a shed, carport, or do almost anything with their property that a homeowner could do in a classic subdivision. Lost Lake does have covenants that require all buildings to have green metal roofs and cedar-colored siding, but each model is unique. Common areas at the park include a private lake for fishing, a pool, tennis courts, and a clubhouse.

Ken and Connie Howe customized their 399-square-foot tiny home outside of Olympia, Washington.

The Howes purchased two wooded adjacent lots, which gives them privacy while still having a sense of community with their neighbors. Their 399-square-foot home has an extra sleeping loft that can accommodate the couple's adult children when they visit. "We have three kids, and they all thought we were a little crazy at first," says Connie. "Our daughter, especially, was worried that she wouldn't have a home to come home to."

The Howes helped their daughter become comfortable with the idea by allowing her to choose the colors and pick the bedspread in the sleeping loft. Each of their kids has embraced their parents' new home. "Our younger son loves it. He'll just go up into the loft and sit. Our oldest son wired our audio and video into the house for us."

The sleeping loft (left) accommodates the Howe's children when they visit; from there, you can see the living room and fireplace (right).

The couple designed their house with retirement in mind. "We are saving a lot for retirement," says Connie. "We also love to travel, so this gives us the flexibility to pick up and go whenever we want."

When they designed the house, they hired Cedar Ridge Industries in Chehalis, Washington, a company that specializes in designing tiny and park model homes. Among some of the customized features the Howes included were placing the washer and dryer under the stairs and installing a central vacuum system. "That makes it so easy to clean, and I don't have to store a vacuum," says Connie. Their lives are now all about Living Large instead of having to maintain a huge house.

## EXPERT TIPS: Sarah Susanka

Living Large is not about square footage alone, but focuses on quality of life. If you don't think a little house fits your lifestyle, you can still design a Not So Big House and Live Large. Sarah Susanka, author of *The Not So Big House*, provided these tips for when you're planning to make Living Large a priority:

- **It doesn't have to be tiny:** There is no one correct size or budget for a Not So Big House, which focuses on the qualities of the space, rather than quantity of square footage. "It's about one-third smaller than you thought you needed, with dollars reappointed from square footage to characteristics that turn a house into a home," says Sarah.

- **Make it personal:** The home first and foremost should be tailored to fit the homeowners and provide them with a sense of livability and comfort they never before thought possible.

- **Design for sustainable living:** A Not So Big House is more than the sum of its parts. It is designed and built to last for generations, and should be energy efficient and sustainable. But most important, it should be beautiful to look at and to live in. We take care of what we find beautiful. The structure is a reflection of its homeowners, and should allow them more time and energy to focus on things that give their lives meaning, rather than impressing others.

- **A good neighbor:** The house should fit into its setting by respecting the views from adjacent homes and blending into the existing streetscape in scale and character.

- **A better floor plan for today:** All the space should be used every day. Many of the rooms do double-duty and will be used for several different activities over the course of the day. Spaces that will be rarely used should be eliminated. With a more open floor plan, adjacent spaces benefit from the presence of each other to give the house greater flexibility and spaciousness without the excess square footage.

- **Interior views:** A Not So Big House features long, diagonal views through adjacent spaces to extend the perceived scale of the house. A strategically placed window or lighted focal point at the end of a view through the house draws the eye toward the farthest point and accentuates the sense of spaciousness.

- **Varying ceiling heights:** Sarah says that we typically think in terms of a floor plan, which shows length and width only, but the third dimension of height is an equally useful tool. It shapes our experience of space and can help make less feel like more. Lower ceiling heights over smaller, less dominant activity areas contrast with the heights of the taller, more important spaces, creating a hierarchy of places, from sheltered and intimate, to open and expansive.

- **Sense of shelter:** A Not So Big House uses a variety of visual cues to provide a degree of separation between open spaces without resorting to a solid wall to accomplish the task. Sheltering devices—such as a raised counter, rug, floating ceiling section, or beam—indicate where one space stops and the next begins, providing a sense of shelter around the activity taking place.

- **Pleasingly proportioned:** The home should feature rooms of appropriate proportioning and that are designed to feel both spacious and intimate. Variations in ceiling height and other architectural elements create rooms that are suitable for groups of people, while still being comfortable for just one or two.

- **Attention to detail:** No matter where you look in a house, everything should be thought through and designed to perfectly support the needs of the people living in the home. Comfort and functionality are qualities designed into a Not So Big House to make it both inspiring to live in and a perfectly crafted container for everyday living.

**LIVING LARGE TIPS:** Finding the Right Size for Your Life

- Decide on a plan based on your square footage now. What rooms do you really use? Which ones are a complete waste? How much space do you think you really need?

- Go primitive camping. Pack only the essentials you need. Make notes about what you used—or didn't—and what you could live without.

- Find spaces to rent for a weekend or a one-to-two-week vacation. Make notes about what you like about the space and what you don't.

- Think about the future. Will you need more space for children or aging relatives? Will you be able to stay in your space when you get older? Make your Living Large dream sustainable for the long term.

- Incorporate your research into your little house design.

# 4

# Culture Shock:
# Adapting to the Reality of Rural Living

*Living Truth: "It is only in the country that we can get to know a person or a book."*

**—CYRIL CONNOLLY, *THE UNQUIET GRAVE***

The continuous pops outside Our Little House sounded like shotgun blasts all around us. In the city, this type of noise would have had us diving underneath the bed for cover, but at Our Little House, we just lay in bed and winced with every loud crack.

It was late at night on January 27, 2009, and a major ice storm was hitting our part of Arkansas. It would eventually blow eastward, leaving an estimated two million people without power. That night, as we listened to what sounded like the entire forest crashing down around us, we wondered if we would have any woods left at all in the morning.

Although major ice storms were rare in Kansas City, we had been through them before. One such storm in the late 1990s knocked out the power in my mom's duplex for a day, maybe two. When I was a kid, we also weathered such a storm in our little bungalow. It was too dangerous to drive—even the few blocks to the local Turner Food Store—and we needed groceries. So Mom, Dad, and I embarked on a trek through the ice and snow. While walking down a hill, my dad fell on his butt, and my mom and I were laughing so hard that we had a difficult time catching up with the tomatoes and oranges rolling down the street.

My memories of ice storms in the city weren't anything like the doomsday predictions the meteorologists in the Ozarks were forecasting in the days preceding the 2009 storm. "I don't understand what the big deal is," I told Fred, our neighbor from Kansas City. Fred and his wife, Rae, had built a home down the road from Our Little House, but they still lived in Kansas City full-time and were planning to head back before the storm hit. "You'd think the world was coming to an end," I said. Fred just smiled. Looking back now, maybe he was more aware of what was coming than I was, as they didn't hesitate to leave for home before the predicted bad weather.

By the time we were lying in bed listening to the landscape crack around us, I thought the world was ending. My dad, who grew up in that small cabin in Clarksville, Arkansas, used to say of his childhood home, "We didn't get much snow, but we would get that ice. . . ." He never elaborated, and I was beginning to understand why. Aside from the many tornado warnings we had been through in our lives, this was by far the worst weather event.

When we rose the next morning, the popping wasn't as frantic as it had been the night before, and it was spaced further apart. In between pops, the woods were eerily silent. We had no power, so there was no hum from the refrigerator or, when we stepped outside, from the heating unit of the Belle Writer's Studio. Thank heavens we had installed an excellent small woodstove in Our Little House for heat.

The ice storm felled many trees.

Upon surveying the damage, we found that we had lost several of our largest trees and many limbs in the onslaught the night before. The hard, rocky clay on these mountains makes deep rooting difficult, so ice can knock over a perfectly healthy tree, roots and all.

We were thankful that none of the trees or limbs had landed on our buildings and that the electrical and phone lines coming from poles into the house and studio were still hanging. The power outage was apparently originating from somewhere up the mountain. For the next five days, we made the best of our situation. Fred and Rae had left us one small generator, which allowed me to send emails to my work contacts, explaining our situation. Somehow, our telephone service was never interrupted. (We were still on dial-up service!)

The generator wasn't big enough to power the large appliances simultaneously, so Dale had to sporadically take the refrigerator off of the generator so we could watch television and get some news. We cooked on the woodstove, which, for about two days, was fun and exciting.

After that, pioneer life became taxing. We brought ice into the tub and let it melt for water to flush the toilet. We took cold sponge baths. A hot bath—unless we wanted to heat the water on the woodstove—was out of the question.

Dale picked up limbs and moved them from the road when he walked the 1.7 miles to the mailbox, which was a slippery proposition. It was hard to walk on the solid sheets of ice and impossible to drive. On day five, we were finally able to make it into town. The destruction we saw was comparable only to tornado damage I had witnessed in a small town near Kansas City when I was covering it for a news story. However, tornados cut a relatively small path of devastation. In this ice storm, the entire landscape had been leveled.

There were power and telephone lines down and power poles broken in half. Trees and limbs had fallen on cars, homes, and across the roads. The entire region was still without power, and for miles, all we could hear was the buzzing of chain saws.

When we got to town, we went into the farm and home store to see if they had any propane for our camp stove or, by some miracle, a larger generator. A crowd had gathered at the store. People were waiting for a half a dozen generators that were supposed to be delivered on a truck that afternoon. But while we were there, the manager announced that the truck wouldn't be able to make it, which didn't make the storm-weary crowd happy. Trucks hadn't been able to access the town for five days, so the local Walmart looked as though looters had come in and taken every loaf of bread and gallon of milk. Pallets that once held huge cartons of bottled water and propane were empty.

We picked up a case of water that was being given out to citizens at the local fire department and returned home. We called Fred and asked him to buy us a larger generator in the city, assuring him we would pay him back when he arrived. Two days later, we were still waiting for our power to be restored. By then, I would have given anything for a hot shower and a dinner that wasn't cooked on the woodstove. On the afternoon of day seven, after coming home from a restaurant in town that had power and having eaten the best hamburger I've ever tasted, I told Dale, "I'm going to go up and check my plants in the studio." I only got about three steps toward the studio when I heard the most wonderful sound—the whir of the studio's heat pump. We had power!

I actually did a little dance in the driveway before running into the house to see if the water was hot enough yet for a bath. Fred brought our generator the next day, which ensured we would never be without power during or after a storm again.

🏠

Despite the occasional hardships of living in the country, we're glad we're so far out here because the county does not have a minimum square footage requirement, as most cities do. At 480 square feet, Our Little House would not have met building codes of many suburban and even rural areas. That is why—with the exception of older homes built in the first half of the twentieth century, before many building codes were enacted—you'll find most tiny homes in rural areas. Our grandparents and great-grandparents generally lived in smaller homes, and many of those homes still exist in older neighborhoods today.

We especially love our home in the summer. We have the mountains and the beautiful woods, as well as access to one of the most gorgeous lakes in the country. Our closest neighbors are my Aunt Kathy and her husband Monty, who live about a quarter mile down the road. We don't consider ourselves antisocial, but having a lot of privacy has its benefits. There is no one on the other side of our driveway to dispute property lines with, as we did once with our neighbors in our split-level. There aren't any kids screaming and splashing in a pool 100 feet away while I'm trying to enjoy a summer afternoon working on my deck.

We really enjoy these benefits of rural living. But we've found the winters to be brutal when the weather gets bad. Even relatively small snow and ice storms can make it extremely dangerous for Dale to get to work. Our road is 1.7 miles of dirt straight up the mountain before hitting blacktop. His 13-mile commute also turns into 30 if he has to take the state highway route instead of the "back way" over more treacherous mountain roads.

The road leading to Our Little House.

Of course, the ice storm wasn't the first time our power went out. I don't think there was a time we came down for our weekend visits before we moved here when we didn't have to reset the clocks from the power at least having flickered. Getting high-speed Internet in a rural area can also be difficult. When we moved here, the only thing our little local rural telephone company offered on our road was dial-up—and this was in 2007!

Several years later, we finally got DSL—at the speed you'd find in cities in the year 2000. Cell phone companies have made it easier by offering data packages to tether cell phones to computers, but the service can be spotty. Satellite offers limited data packages, and if you exceed your data for the month, it either runs extremely slowly or they shut it off, which is something I cannot have happen when I run a business from home.

🏠

The ice storm of 2009 also wasn't the first time we felt like strangers in a strange land, living a life completely different than the one we had left in the city. The 300 miles that separated our rural life from our city life might not have seemed like much, but because they separated a Midwestern city from the rural South, language and customs felt as foreign to us as some we encountered on our trip to Germany.

Although my East Coast friends tell me that I have a Southern accent—probably a little Midwestern twang mixed with my dad's Arkansas drawl—I could hardly understand some of the folks in our newly adopted hometown, much to my embarrassment and their annoyance.

When I first went into a gas station after moving here, with my *Chicago Tribune* baseball cap and Kansas City Royals T-shirt, the woman behind the counter asked if I was from Chicago or Kansas City. (There are many transplants from both cities here.) I smiled, "Kansas City." She smiled back and said something in such a deep Southern drawl that I had to ask her to repeat it three times. Finally, she slowed down and enunciated her words very carefully, "Which. Pump. Are. You. At?"

That incident happened the same week that I asked the butcher at the local grocery if they had organic, grass-fed beef. He looked at me like I was from another planet and said, "Nope. But we have it processed *the regular way.*" If that wasn't enough to make me feel like we had indeed found the big changes from city life that we were seeking, a woman working at the tiny local library told me when I inquired about a book on philanthropy by President Bill Clinton (I'm an American history fanatic and read books by politicians and world leaders of all stripes) that they "probably wouldn't be gettin' that one; no one much likes him 'round here."

When our first autumn rolled around, I was excited to experience some of the local festivals that the Ozarks are known for. A town nearby has one called the Turkey Trot Festival. I called my aunt to see if she wanted to go with me. "Um, you do know what they do at that festival, don't you?" I didn't. "They throw live turkeys from a plane, and if they survive, the kids chase them down and catch them."

I think I was still in a state of disbelief when I read the next day in the paper that live wild turkeys are indeed thrown from a plane to "fly, glide or plummet to the ground." As it turns out, wild turkeys can fly, but usually at low altitudes for short periods of time. It's unknown how many of the turkeys tossed from the plane at the Turkey Trot Festival haven't been able to right themselves and have crashed into buildings, cars, or concrete, but a video given to PETA by a local resident and subsequently posted online showed at least one.

The local chamber of commerce, which sponsors the festival, long ago distanced itself from the turkey drop. Local officials claim not to endorse the pilot of the small plane. PETA offered a reward that year for anyone who turned in the "phantom pilot" who flew the plane. Apparently his identity is a closely guarded town secret, especially since the FAA actually does have strict rules about throwing objects from planes.

As it turns out, that particular custom is bigger than the national turkey-calling contest and the naming of the turkey royalty in the pageant, and the townspeople were livid when an outside animal rights organization threatened a decades-old tradition. The majority of local natives strongly defend the drop, arguing that the festival adds to the local economy and that the majority of turkeys survive unscathed. I'm not at all a PETA supporter, but I'm an animal lover and can't stand the idea of a bird possibly splatting on a building after plummeting from a plane. But by that time, I knew not to discuss a lot of my "big city beliefs" with local natives. Still, I thought I was safe telling an acquaintance who is a fellow vegetarian and transplant, how I felt about the turkey drop. I knew she had a young child, but didn't think she would allow her kid to be exposed to turkeys possibly splatting on the streets. "Well, I just feel sorry for the kids. They all look forward to it every year," she said.

I was more than a little stunned. "Why in the world would you want your child to think that using animals like that is okay?" I asked. She smiled, "In a small town, you have to pick your battles. I just don't think this one is worth fighting."

It took me a few years to understand that no matter how long you live in a small town, you'll always be perceived as a "newcomer" or "outsider," especially if you're not on board with the town's long-standing beliefs, customs, and traditions. I now understand that the woman was giving her child that sense of belonging in what is now the child's hometown.

The majority of people born and raised here don't care how the turkey drop is viewed from the outside world or to folks who have moved here from that world. Like us, most of the people I know here try to ignore the controversy and just skip the festival.

In 2011, the FAA did warn the "phantom pilot" through the media that it would monitor the festivities and anyone caught dropping turkeys from a plane would lose their pilot's license. That stopped the 60-plus-year tradition for a few years, but after the controversy died down, the drop resumed in 2015, much to the delight of a cheering crowd.

A nagging feeling that I had previously seen a story about turkeys falling from the sky was verified when someone pointed me to an episode of the '70s sitcom *WKRP in Cincinnati*, in which the character Arthur Carlson planned a live turkey drop as a promotion. "As God is my witness, I thought turkeys could fly," he exclaims after the disastrous event, which used farmed turkeys, which cannot fly. I've never been able to verify it, but there is a rumor that the episode was written with the Arkansas Turkey Trot Festival in mind, as one of the writers on the show was a native son. However, this may be as true as the rumor that the movie *Deliverance* was filmed on the Buffalo River near here. (According to many publications and websites dedicated to Hollywood history, the movie was actually filmed in other parts of the South.)[20]

Once we got past some of the culture shock of moving to a rural area, life in the country became easygoing, and it's mostly a friendly place. On our back roads, for example, people wave at you, whether they know you or not. I even started noticing the different kinds of acknowledgments given by passing drivers. There is the slight head nod, the little salute, the one-finger wave (that's index finger off of the steering wheel, not that *other* one-finger wave), and the full-hand wave. Dale typically does the head nod, while I prefer that index-finger acknowledgment.

Music-on-the-square events on weekend evenings during the summer give us something to do. Just like when we were growing up in our small community of Turner, I've become familiar with the different owners and employees at our favorite stores. Grocery shopping becomes more enjoyable when you know your grocer by name, and he or she will order something for you if they don't have it in stock.

Sue Smith Moak, who lives in this 464-square-foot cabin in the Texas Hill Country, knows firsthand the importance of relying on neighbors when living in a remote area.

While the neighbors aren't close in proximity, there's the knowledge that many of them would be there if needed. The volunteer fire department fosters a sense of community. One of our neighbors, who volunteers for the fire department, dropped off a case of water for us at the top of the mountain during the ice storm, before we could get to town. When we lose a neighbor, we gather with food and condolences for the family after services at the community building. Folks also gather there for weekly card games and occasional fund-raisers. In the event of tragedy—when someone has been injured in a car wreck, or a child has a terrible illness—the local community rallies.

Other small house dwellers have found the same to be true of their rural communities. Sue Smith Moak, 65, lives in her 464-square-foot cabin on 54 acres in the rural Texas Hill Country. She and her husband, Rick, bought the property 25 years ago as a place to retire. They had previously lived in Houston, but both loved country living. Sue retired first, while Rick stayed in Houston, commuting to the property on vacations and weekends until he could retire. When Sue retired, they didn't get typical pets like cats or dogs. Sue says it was always Rick's dream to have longhorns, so they got two—named Woodrow and Gus—for their pasture. "They're treated just like pets," Sue says.

Sue and Rick built what they could afford and thought if they ever needed more space, they could add on later. However, little house living was an idea Sue picked up from her father-in-law. He lived in a large house, but as he got older, he closed off most of the house and only used the living room, kitchen, and bathroom. This made Sue realize that, especially as they grew older, they would need less space to live.

Sue lives about 15 miles outside of town, but like us, she's found that if help is needed, you depend on your neighbors first in the country, rather than on city or county services. "Our neighbors have a call system to alert anyone to things we need to know, like a man on the run from law enforcement or the power company in the neighborhood doing work, or a predator killing livestock," Sue says.

Sadly, Sue's husband, Rick, passed away from a sudden heart attack while at the cabin just before Thanksgiving weekend in 2014. Sue said it was her neighbors and the local sheriff's department that helped perform CPR on Rick before the paramedics arrived.

Sue said the woman at the local post office offered any help Sue needed after she lost Rick, and the clerk at the feed store offered to deliver feed to Sue's house. "The funeral home made a donation in Rickie's name, as they do for all those they serve, to the building fund for the local historical museum. These small-town ways both surprise and humble me," Sue says. "We have a wild game dinner each November that benefits local charities. People donate everything from venison to alligator meat."

Health care is also something important to consider when moving to a rural area. When I was 40 years old, I had to have a major surgery to repair damage to my stomach and chest that a horse inflicted when it threw me back four feet. Kansas City is a large enough metropolitan area that it has some of the finest health-care facilities in the world. The surgeon who operated on me there was ranked one of the best in the country for that particular surgery.

When disclosing my medical history here, I've actually had to explain the surgery I had to doctors who have never heard of it. Thus far, we've received adequate health care in our rural area, but we've never suffered a debilitating illness or injury while here. Many rural hospitals lack trauma centers, and first responders, who are typically part of the volunteer fire department (VFD), are sometimes slow to arrive, depending on where they're coming from.

When we first obtained our homeowner's insurance, our agent told us it was a requirement to pay the annual fee to the VFD. "It's really a formality," he told us in a deep Southern drawl. "It gives them money to buy the hotdogs," he added, smiling. That isn't to disparage the wonderful volunteers who train and generously donate their time—I have the utmost respect for what they do for rural communities—but a volunteer-staffed rural emergency response team generally isn't as well staffed or well equipped as a city emergency team staffed full-time by paid employees.

We pay our VFD dues and have taken out insurance that covers medical flights to a larger hospital should we experience a severe health crisis. Nonetheless, as we grow older in Our Little House, health care will continue to be a concern.

Living in a small home in the country isn't just for retirees. Raising a young family in the country can be a great experience, according to Hari Berzins, who lived for four years with her husband, Karl, and two children, Ella (12) and Archer (10), in a 336-square-foot tiny home. Their tiny house is cozy, but offers a full kitchen, as well as room for the family to sit and eat together. Two sleeping lofts that run the full length of the space and give Hari and Karl their own space. The children share a loft. The home sits on three acres outside of Floyd, Virginia.

Their story begins in suburban Florida, where they were one of the many families who lost their business and home during the Great Recession. They decided to build a

The Berzinses lived in a 336-square-foot tiny home in rural Virginia, allowing children Ella and Archer to develop a deep appreciation for nature.

tiny home that they could finance using the cash they had—without a mortgage—and began looking for rural property in the Mid-Atlantic region. "We met in Colorado and knew we wanted to be in the mountains," Hari says. "I have a cousin in Roanoke, and she mentioned this area. We began exploring places online, and it was a long process of narrowing it down and choosing the right property for us."

Choosing a place where the kids could run and play was important to the family. "The kids play together and engage in pretend play all of the time," says Hari. "They have hideouts in the woods and build forts." Hari says that living in a rural area has helped her children develop a sense of being a kid, something many suburban and city children no longer enjoy because of the perceived dangers. In fact, a poll conducted by Reasons-Rupe in 2014 found that 63 percent of adults surveyed said that 12 years old is too young to leave children unsupervised in parks, and 82 percent of those polled said that it should be against the law for children under nine to play in a park unsupervised.[21]

Hari says living in the country has helped her children develop a very deep appreciation for nature. "When it was below zero one day, they followed the creek to the source. They said it really isn't winter if the creek doesn't freeze. I love that they know this kind of stuff," says Hari. "They know where to look for daffodils and when things are supposed to bloom. It has given them a very good sense of place."

For Dale and me, there are certain city things we still miss, such as a nice selection of good ethnic food and coffee shops. However, I've been able to solve most of those issues by carefully planning shopping trips, learning to cook the dishes I miss (I've even cooked a traditional Ethiopian dish, an exotic choice for this Midwestern family), and buying a coffee grinder and good coffee to make at home. Eating out and having a coffee house coffee is now a treat when we go to a bigger town or visit the city.

Aside from the brutal Ozark Mountain winters, we've found rural life typically fun, if a bit quirky. It isn't so quirky that we have a crazy mailman who throws mail at us and cackles as he drives away as the one did in the popular 1980s Chevy Chase film *Funny Farm*, but we've learned to mostly adapt to our new rural culture.

We can also enjoy our dogs and our hobbies. I love to ride our four-wheeler on our rural road and Dale likes to target practice in our yard, typically without worry of disturbing our neighbors or adhering to code regulations found in city life.

Even the ice storm had its eventual benefits. It provided us with enough felled trees for years of warm heat from the stove in Our Little House.

---

**LIVING LARGE TIPS:** Adjusting to Rural Life in Your Little Home

- Get to know your area before moving there. If you're accustomed to shopping in large city supermarkets, keep in mind that many rural areas will not have large stores with a diverse selection of foods.

Before our area got a natural-foods store, we would take coolers on our trips to the larger cities for big shopping trips.

- If you live in an area that's subject to harsh winters, plan your home as if you're off grid, with a woodstove for heat and cooking if you lose power, a generator, and, ideally, a four-wheeler or tractor to move mounds of snow. It may be awhile, if ever, before the county digs you out. Be sure to plan storage for extra food supplies, in case you are ever iced or snowed in. It's also a good idea to have extra gasoline and basic auto knowledge/supplies on hand and a plan in place to get to town in case your car breaks down.

- Finally, if you work from home or are retired, ask yourself if you're *really* the type of person who can be isolated from the outside world for periods of time. Vacationing in a rural area is much different than living in one, especially during long winters in a very small space.

Dale says since he works all day, he really doesn't have time for cabin fever, but if you're home all of the time like I am, you'll be looking for ways to avoid the winter blues. Here are some things I do that help:

- **Dog-walking:** We might not be able to get out on the water, but the weather here is nice enough most of the time to bundle up and take a long walk on our country road.

- **Yoga:** Due to some back and stomach issues, I do chair yoga and some standing poses to help my balance. This type of yoga takes very little room and helps keep me centered.

- **Reading:** I have enough magazines and books to keep me busy for the next 50 years.

- **Writing:** Sure, I write as a profession, but it's different from my creative writing. I keep a gratitude journal daily to remind myself of how fortunate we are.

- **Photography:** There are always photos to snap of the dogs or the wildlife, and when I want candid shots of wildlife, I walk our wildlife camera deep into the woods to see what I can capture. It's typically deer, squirrels, raccoons, and crows. I did capture a very healthy large coyote on the camera and hope to get a mountain lion and a bear someday.

- **Adult coloring books:** This is the best craze to hit our country, as it allows those of us with little artistic talent to still create something beautiful. I get together with my aunt and a couple of neighbors and we have coloring book parties, complete with food and libations (no boys allowed!). It's true what they say about it being a stress reliever.

- **Antiquing:** We live in a resort area, so there are many antique malls in the towns all over the region. Dale and I don't buy anything (we don't need anything else), but we still love to look.

- **Going to the movies:** Our small town has two movie theaters. We can lose ourselves in a movie waiting for spring.

- **Bowling:** Dale always beats me, but I still enjoy an afternoon of throwing a ball and killing pins.

- **Volunteering:** The fall leading up to the holiday season is a great time to find a charity to help. If you don't have anyone to celebrate the holidays with, serving food to seniors or those less fortunate is a quick pick me up.

- **Visiting the local museums and park visitor centers:** We have many parks and a large visitor center on the lake, which doesn't close in the winter. They have some of the most interesting programs in the winter, including educational presentations on the eagles that frequent the lake.

# 5

# So You Have a Love/Hate Thing with Credit:
## Taking on a Debt-Free Mind-Set

*Living Truth:* "*Rather go to bed without dinner than to rise in debt.*"
—BENJAMIN FRANKLIN

We sensed it was coming, but we hoped we were wrong. We contracted to have the Belle Writer's Studio built in the summer of 2008, just before we realized the economy was headed into a serious freefall. That summer, gasoline prices hit a record average high of $4 per gallon,[22] which was of particular concern for Dale's employer. If people can't afford gasoline, they don't buy boats.

Overtime was eliminated, and several of Dale's coworkers were let go. We knew that since Dale had been on the job less than a year he would likely be one of the first to go if a mass layoff happened.

That day arrived in mid-November, one year and one week after (to the day) he was hired. At the time, contractors were putting the finishing touches on my writer's studio, but my writing business was beginning to crumble. I had focused my writing in the area of my passion—print newspapers. I had a few magazine clients and some trade newsletters and magazines, but 80 percent of my business was in print newspapers. Digital media had already struck a blow to print newspapers, and when the economy crumbled, it was the final death knell for many.

I loved working for newspapers, covering community news, crime, and politics. A mentor at *The Kansas City Star* once told me that I had a gift for writing engaging features, which I also loved to do. For that reason, I had been slow to develop an online writing résumé. In 2008, in a matter of weeks, I became a dinosaur in my profession, with little experience in new media.

The only positive side to our situation was that Dale could draw unemployment from his previous employer in Kansas, where the payments were a little higher than in Arkansas. He also had plenty of time to do the inside finishing work on the studio and some other projects around the house, such as painting the bedroom. I admit, I did enjoy having him home. I had a personal chef cooking my lunches and, for the first time in my life, a housekeeper.

We had secured financing for the studio before the economic collapse. By the end of November, I was networking with colleagues and former editors and sending letters of introduction and queries to online outlets. After 10 years in the business, I was essentially starting from scratch.

Dale was also busy submitting his résumé and filing job applications, but as John Mellencamp sings in "Small Town," there really was little opportunity (for jobs), especially when the country was sinking into the worst economic disaster since the Great Depression. Dale's employer, one of the biggest in the region, had laid off hundreds. In a small town where many folks work for one company, the dominoes began to fall immediately, and it became very noticeable.

As Christmas neared that year, we could walk into our town's Walmart, even as late as December 23, and find it eerily empty. The festive holiday carols playing over the loudspeaker made it seem like we were in one of those science-fiction movies in which the world was suddenly wiped of humans and the music was playing for no one. The only day-care center in town closed. (Why would people need day care if they weren't working?) Eventually, the recession also claimed the independently owned pharmacy, two grocery stores, and several restaurants in nearby towns.

We thought it would only last the winter, but as spring 2009 approached, it was evident that the boat plant wouldn't be calling workers back anytime soon. Dale finally landed a job at a local farm and lawn equipment supplier, where he used his mechanical skills to work on lawn equipment and tractors. The pay was considerably less than he had earned previously, but we were grateful that he found a job before his unemployment expired. Fortunately, he liked the job and the people.

In the meantime, I was rebuilding my business, but it was slow going. We had to begin using credit cards to meet some financial obligations. We still had a nearly $600 monthly truck payment, and we also had to pay for our own health insurance. COBRA was too expensive, but a federal plan designed to help people who had lost their jobs allowed us to keep Dale's plan from his former employer and pay a discounted amount, which still added up to $360 a month. We had auto and life insurance payments, the ever-rising costs of groceries and gas (Dale's new employer was now 45 minutes away, as opposed to just 20 minutes), and a new unsecured loan for the studio. More troubling to us was a mortgage on Our Little House that was on a five-year balloon plan that had come due again in 2008. We renewed it but were making little, if any, headway on the principal.

Believing that we could rebuild our savings, we'd used every penny we had to dig the well the previous year and build a new outbuilding; what was left went toward building the studio. The last of our emergency fund went to purchase the generator during the ice storm.

We had never been in this situation before. If Dale's attitude about jobs had been translated to the stock market, he would have been one of the most conservative investors who ever played the game. After his 1984 layoff from his union job at the meat company, he turned down several opportunities over the years that would have paid more but were more likely to involve layoffs. He stuck with his job at the landfill because it was safe. When we moved, he made sure to check into the history of the boat company, and we believed at the time that it was a relatively safe opportunity as well.

My history, on the collections side of the credit industry, also ensured that I was reasonably layoff-proof when it came to economic downturns. When I began my freelance writing business, it went amazingly well for the first decade. I always seemed to be in the right place at the right time, and if I lost an opportunity, another typically came knocking before the end of the day.

We weren't rich, but we were comfortable and could always meet our obligations. When the Great Recession hit, however, I didn't know what to do, except for what my mother had always described as "robbing Peter to pay Paul." I handled the finances and would often lie awake at night trying to figure out what I could juggle to meet various due dates. Our credit had always been impeccable; it was something that was important to both of us, and we didn't want to see it ruined. My dad always used to say, "In the end, all you have is your good name. Never ruin it." For us, our good name was our credit.

During the 18 months of our own financial crisis, I clipped coupons. We only ate out once a month, and that was only with a "buy one dinner, get the other free" coupon at a chain Tex-Mex restaurant. The only trips we made home to Kansas City were if I really needed to travel for my business.

We took advantage of offers from the bank to skip truck payments and add them to the end of the loan. We were finally able to get a loan modification on it for a period of time. Some payments were late, and for the first time we began to receive collection calls. The lesson I had learned so early in life, that "robbing Peter to pay Paul" was not sustainable, came back to haunt me.

As 2009 rolled into 2010, Dale was laid off again. He was in a job that was seasonal — no one was concerned about lawn equipment in the winter. With the economy in the tank, many people were waiting to see what the New Year would bring before having their tractors repaired.

Dale was back on unemployment, and this time he had to draw from Arkansas, which paid considerably less than the maximum amount in Kansas. The economy was starting to show a glimmer of hope by that time, and some employers around our area were beginning to hire again. The problem was that the available positions were low-paying, nearly minimum-wage factory jobs. Dale is a skilled mechanic, but after applying to companies that might need his labor and not receiving a call back, he ended up taking one of those $7.50-an-hour jobs working forty hours a week. He worked an additional part-time job at the farm and home store, assembling lawn equipment and grills. The pay was about the same, so in approximately fourteen months, he had gone from landing a pretty good job in his field to having to work seventy hours a week for less money and no benefits.

The man who hired him at the factory told him there was room for advancement, and Dale initially felt encouraged that he might be able to work into a second career. But it wasn't long before we both became discouraged again. Dale's take-home pay from his full-time job was not even enough to pay for gasoline for our truck or groceries each week, much less pay the rest of our bills.

My business was still in recovery, and we sank further into debt. By May, as Dale grew more tired and stressed from the extended hours (we aren't, after all, young adults anymore) and I became more tired and stressed from sleepless nights, working long hours to help rebuild my business, and juggling bills, I told him it was time to give up. I had never wanted to sell Our Little House—the land was originally purchased with money my mom received from selling the Wilson House, and to me, it was the last of what remained of her dream. Our Little House had become our dream, but I was afraid we were slipping to the point of no return. I feared we would end up filing for bankruptcy, and it felt like we were drowning.

The housing market took a sharp dive during the Great Recession, though. Homes all over our area stood vacant, with foreclosure notices on the doors and "for sale" signs in the yard. As families moved away, the local school district lost so many students and state aid that it was listed by the state as being in financial distress. We didn't know what our house and acreage were valued at, but I made an appointment with a real estate agent to come out and give us an idea of what he thought we could get for it.

A balloon mortgage is one in which you basically pay the interest, with the balloon or balance coming due on a specific date. It was the only mortgage we had been able to get with a local bank due to the size of our house. Because we could never come up with a large payment for the principle, it was impossible to make any real progress on the balance. We had been making interest payments for the past six-and-a-half years. I knew we probably wouldn't make enough from the sale to buy another home someplace else and that, in fact, we would be lucky just to break even.

We didn't know where we would go with four dogs in tow, but we had to go somewhere Dale could find good-paying work in his field, and maybe where I could even work while I rebuilt my business. I had applied for jobs near our town in the previous months, but they were so low-paying that it didn't make sense for me to give up my writing income to have yet another expensive commute to town.

I made the appointment with the realtor for a Wednesday afternoon in the beginning of May. That Tuesday, Dale's former supervisor and friend at the boat company told him they would call him back. He wouldn't be in the diesel shop at first, but to keep us from moving out of town, they would put him in the factory until business picked up enough for them to rehire him as a mechanic.

We had barely escaped total financial ruin. We were thousands of dollars in credit-card debt, but we were able to hold onto our home. Back in 2007, we had felt we received a message from the universe when our Kansas City split-level sold within five days, and this time, we felt like it had aligned once again to tell us that Our Little House was where we needed to be.

♦

Many Americans lost their homes during the recession, including Hari and Karl Berzins. In 2007, the couple opened a restaurant in St. Cloud, Florida. Just a year later, the recession hit Florida hard. On top of the economic "hurricane" depleting people's discretionary budgets, Tropical Storm Fay swept through Florida in August 2008 and was the death knell for the Berzinses' restaurant. "Business started slowing down before the storm, but after that damage, it came to a screeching halt," Hari says. They found it impossible to hold on. They had to close their business, and then their 1,500-square-foot home went into foreclosure.

"We decided that we didn't want to play the financial game anymore," says Hari. "We wanted to live outside of the credit system." They took what money they had and began building what they could afford, which was a 168-square-foot home on a trailer. The couple decided to put the home on a trailer because they didn't want to stay in Florida. Instead, they wanted to be in the mountains, so they began looking for property. They found a Virginia property online, paid cash, and moved their tiny home to its new location.

Once they moved, they realized how unique having four people in such a tiny home is, so they started their website, TinyHouseFamily.com. Hari is a teacher, but on the side, she blogs about their experiences in a tiny home. Also, they both teach an online class on becoming debt-free. In addition, Karl builds tiny homes for others. For the Berzinses, their first little home on wheels was a means to an eventual end: They planned on building a larger home on their Virginia acreage at some point in the future. The couple's two children, Archer and Ella, were 6 and 8 when they moved to their tiny home in 2011, and they knew the brother and sister would eventually need separate space. Thanks to Karl's construction experience, he built their larger home himself.

Their bigger house was originally planned for 750 square feet, but it had to be expanded to meet code requirements (including needing a stationary staircase rather than just a ladder leading to loft space) to a 1,400-square-foot design. It is no longer a tiny home—or even a particularly small one—but Hari says the important thing is that it is mortgage-free and allows the family to remain on their rural property.

While they are now living in a larger space, the Berzinses wouldn't trade their tiny house experience for anything—because it taught the family the important lesson of Living Large. They learned how to live simply and with only what's necessary. They also realized that extra space is sometimes needed to follow passions and enjoy life to the fullest. The new home will allow Ella, an artist, room for her art supplies and projects, and will allow Archer, a musician, room for his instruments. "It's been a long, slow journey, and we're ready," says Hari. "It will add a lot of happiness and new elements to our lives."

The Berzinses moved into their larger house at the end of the summer in 2015. They kept their tiny home and are renting it out as a short-term accommodation. "People who follow our blog would like to try it and see how it feels," says Hari.

Family dinners like this one are tiny home memories that will be forever treasured by the Berzinses.

Many others suffered financial losses during the Great Recession too. Mary Dunning was in her late 50s when her lifelong dream of owning a successful horse stable and boarding business went south. The six acres of land she purchased in 2005 came with a 2,000 square-foot farmhouse, a 32-stall horse barn, and indoor riding arena. It was located just outside of Kansas City in a rural bedroom community. Unfortunately, even its proximity to city dwellers who might want to board horses didn't help Mary's business.

Mary had a full-time job, but it wasn't enough to keep up the huge payments on the property. "That was right before everything fell apart, and no one was spending money on horses," says Mary. "It was my dream to oversee a successful horse business, but the timing just wasn't right and I watched as my dream became a nightmare. It eventually resulted in foreclosure that forced me into downsizing and readjusting my dream."

In July 2011, Mary moved from her rambling farmhouse into a 380-square-foot cabin on 28 acres, which she paid for by withdrawing money from her retirement account. "The biggest reward, by far, has been lack of debt and the ability to live life on my own terms, not the terms of a bank or mortgage company," Mary says. "If I can't pay for something, I don't buy it."

Mary was also very glad she made her move before being laid off from her longtime job in 2013. In addition, she had to undergo shoulder surgery, which has put her on permanent disability. However, Mary didn't give up her dream of having a business that profits from the land. She now has seven goats and runs a small goat-milk soap business, Capra Body Works, from her home.

The soap business required her to expand her home as she needed a separate room for it. "I have five dogs and two cats, and couldn't have the hair getting into the soap," Mary says. With another withdrawal from her retirement account, she added extra space for her business. Her little home is now 832 square feet—but she is still living debt-free.

🏠

An economic downturn isn't the only event that can drive people to tiny homes. In 2014, Ariel McGlothin, 28, was living in Jackson, Wyoming, with her roommate. "The rent there is insanely expensive," says Ariel. "Our place sold, so we had to find another place to live."

Ariel discovered that finding an affordable rental was almost impossible in the pricey resort town, so she initially toyed with the idea of living in a camper van. Although Ariel—the oldest of seven children—grew up in a large home in Pennsylvania, her family was frugal, growing most of their own food and sewing all of their own clothes.

"I knew I could live in a small space. I've lived in cars while road-tripping and lived in a 20-square-foot tent while backpacking," she explains. She began researching camping vans, and that's when she learned about the tiny house movement and Colorado Springs-based Tumbleweed Tiny Houses, which builds tiny houses on wheels. "I wanted to make sure that I had a place to park it, and when I found an amazing location on a friend's property, we got it going," says Ariel.

She also needed financing, which can be a challenge with small homes. However, Tumbleweed's tiny homes are on wheels, and the company is licensed as a recreational-vehicle dealer. This allowed Ariel to secure financing on her home as a recreational vehicle through her credit union. Once her financing was set, she traveled to Colorado Springs to work with the company on customizing her tiny home.

The 229-square-foot tiny-on-a-trailer is completely off grid, using solar power and a gas generator to help during the dead of winter. Ariel made sure she had plenty of kitchen space for cooking, which is one of her passions. The home has a full set of stairs with hidden storage in each step, and the house is even large enough to accommodate a few houseplants.

Ariel McGlothin's 229-square-foot tiny home was built on a trailer and is completely off-grid.

Although Ariel took out a loan for her tiny house, she says the monthly payment is still less than what she paid in rent. This has given her the freedom to work only three days a week most of the time during the summer, leaving her more time to pursue her passions of outdoor sports and activities. "I do work extra in the winter so I can pay more on my loan, which I plan on having paid off in four years," says Ariel.

Ariel also saves money using a system long forgotten by most of today's society: bartering. She loves cooking and apparently is a pretty good at it, as she barters meals for both the rent on the land she lives on, as well as for her gym membership. Although her home has a shower, she doesn't have a permanent water source, so she fills her water tank manually from a neighbor's house and conserves water by showering at her gym.

As the Berzinses, Mary, and Ariel illustrate, one aspect of Living Large is about learning to manage your finances and being creative so you can live your dream and pursue your passions.

---

**EXPERT TIPS:** Beverly Harzog

Becoming debt-free is a long process, according to Beverly Harzog, consumer credit expert and author of *The Debt Escape Plan: How to Free Yourself From Credit Card Balances, Boost Your Credit Score, and Live Debt-Free.* Beverly offers this advice on creating your own debt escape plan:

- **If you're in credit-card debt,** the first thing to do is stop using credit cards. It's very difficult to get out of debt if you keep adding to your credit-card balances.

- **There are a few different strategies** you can use to pay off your balances. If you still have excellent credit, consider getting a balance transfer card. With one of these cards, you'll have the chance to pay down—and maybe even pay off—your debt while paying zero interest. Balance transfer cards offer a zero percent introductory offer for a set period of time, usually around twelve to eighteen months. It's a golden opportunity to pay off debt while saving money on interest.

- **But if this isn't an option for you,** make a list of your credit cards with interest rates and balances. Paying off debt successfully has a lot to do with choosing a strategy that works with your money "personality." If you're a person who needs a quick psychological boost to stay motivated, then the snowball method might work best. With this strategy, you pay off the card with the smallest balance first. Throw as much money as you can at the target balance and pay the minimums on your other credit cards. When you pay off the target balance, move to the next smallest balance. With the snowball method, you pay more interest, but some people prefer this approach because they get a quick win. Reducing the number of balances they have keeps them motivated.

- **Another strategy is called the avalanche method.** List your debts starting with the card that has the highest interest rate (APR). Again, throw as much money as you can at the target balance and pay the minimums on the other credit cards. When you pay off the target balance, you move to the card with the next highest interest rate. With this method, you pay less interest, so this approach saves the most money. If you get an adrenaline rush from saving money, this strategy is a better choice for you.

- **Where do you get the extra money** to throw at the target debt? Examine your budget and decide where you can eliminate or downsize an expense. Consider a second job, or refinancing your car to get a lower monthly payment. In other words, explore all your options and decide which ones work for you.

- **Credit-card debt is toxic debt,** so your priority is to get rid of those balances. It's more important to work on building an emergency fund while you're getting out of debt than it is to save for a major purchase right now. When you pay off that last dollar of debt, you'll feel amazing. Then you can focus on saving for your goal. Put the money you once applied to monthly credit-card payments into an account that you've started for your dream tiny home.

- **Unless you have a credit card with a high annual fee** or you have a shopping addiction, it's a good idea to keep your accounts open. This is because it helps you maintain an excellent credit score. An excellent score saves you money on health insurance, car insurance, mortgage rates, and more. Also, you never know when you might have a financial emergency and need to carry a balance for a few months. Another good reason to keep active credit accounts is because employers look at credit reports. Fair or not, employers assume that those who have excellent credit will be more responsible employees. Keep in mind that you'll need to use the cards once per month or the issuer might decide to close your account. As long as you pay your bill in full each month, it won't cost you anything.

"If you're debt-free, you're already ahead of most people, and you have a great opportunity to start saving for a goal, such as a small house or land," says Beverly. "After you choose your goal, estimate what the cost will be so you have a concrete number to shoot for. The amount might seem daunting, but unless you're living paycheck-to-paycheck, it's possible to find extra money in your current budget."

Beverly offers this advice on saving for your land and little home:

- **Take a long look at your budget,** especially the variable expenses. These are the expenses where you can more easily find a little wiggle room. Go through each expense and question whether or not you need to spend the entire amount you have listed. Now, as you do this, keep in mind that while you do have to make a few sacrifices, you don't have to give up everything you love. Saving money is a lot like dieting. If you decide you won't eat chocolate until you lose 10 pounds, you'll probably end up eating chocolate by the end of the first week. So make sure you still allow yourself a few small splurges now and then so you can enjoy life.

- **Even if you can only find an extra $20 here and there,** it all adds up over time. If you really can't find much money in your budget, then think about taking on a second job. If you've got kids or already work a lot of hours, that might not be a realistic option for you.

- **It's a good idea to set up a special account** for your goal so the money doesn't get mixed in with your main account. Some folks use high-yield online savings accounts for this purpose. Once you decide how much you can contribute each month to this account, stick with it unless you experience a financial emergency. As you watch your savings grow and you get closer to having enough money to fulfill your dream, you'll feel very motivated to stay on track with your savings goal.

---

### LIVING LARGE TIPS: Staying Debt-Free

- When building or moving into your little house—especially if it is in a rural area and you will need to work—it is very important to take the advice of financial experts and always keep at least six months of living expenses saved, just in case.

- It is extremely difficult to get a traditional fixed-rate mortgage on a little home. It took us 18 months to finally refinance Our Little House from our balloon-rate mortgage into a traditional fixed-rate mortgage, which we hope to pay off soon. You may be able to get a loan for an RV if your tiny home is on wheels and the builder classifies its homes as recreational vehicles. The headache of finding a mortgage for a little house is even more incentive to try to do it debt-free.

# 6

# The Clutter of Our Lives:

## Getting Rid of the Stuff that Prevents You from Living Large

*Living Truth:* *"The ability to simplify means to eliminate the unnecessary so that the necessary may speak."*

**—Hans Hoffman**

"That can't be the truck," I told Dale as a neighbor from Arkansas pulled up in front of our split-level in Kansas City. It was 2007, and we had hired him to help us move. My aunt's husband, Monty, had told us the truck was big enough to haul all our stuff for the 300-mile journey to Our Little House.

It probably seemed like a big truck to him, but it was the same size truck that professional moving truck rental companies recommend for a one- or two-bedroom apartment. We had a three-bedroom house, a two-car garage, and a 10-by-12-foot storage shed, all full of 17 years of accumulation. We had spent the prior few weeks going through our belongings, pitching and donating as much as we could. But at that time I believed I'd eventually have a 1,000-square-foot home on our lake property, so we kept everything we loved that was still functional.

Let our experience be the road map for what *not* to do with all of your stuff when you're moving to a little house.

I had, in fact, become my mother, having over time developed an unhealthy and unsustainable relationship with my belongings. By saving all that stuff, I was trying to hold onto what was left of my childhood, which had ended so abruptly at age 17 when my dad died. Also, many of the items had belonged to my mother or grandmother, or had been given to me by my great-aunt. The stuff my mom had kept for years was already in storage. I couldn't yet let go of her things, especially, because letting go of them felt too much like letting go of her.

When our neighbor from Arkansas pulled up in front of the house and we realized we couldn't possibly get our house full of stuff into the truck and two trailers, I sat on our deck and cried. When I recovered, I went down to the storage facility and rented another large unit close to the one we had for my mom's stuff. Next, we had to decide what to put in storage and what we needed at Our Little Lake House.

Don't follow our road map. We spent the next fourteen months paying over $250 per month for the storage units, plus approximately another $1,000 to rent a moving truck and hire guys to help us lift the heavier items when we got to Arkansas. The total amounted to nearly $5,000 that could have been better spent. A year later, we spent another $20,000 constructing the metal storage building on our property.

Eight years later, most of that stuff still sits unused in that building on our property. Some of the wood furniture has gathered mold. It's a shame, not only because no one is using it but also because some of it has actually been damaged—in addition to costing us thousands of dollars in storage and moving expenses. I get a sick feeling every time I open the door to that building. It continues to clutter our lives physically and mentally.

Most folks I've talked to who have moved to a tiny home will say that the most challenging aspect of transitioning to a smaller space is letting go—letting go of sentimental items, collections, and overall clutter. It's been one of the biggest challenges for me, particularly since my mother died just a few months prior to our move.

I now realize that I do not—and never will—need her good china, her dining room table set, her large, gold-framed, sofa-size painting of the French countryside that she bought specifically for the space above the mantel in the Wilson House (and that she took with her to every apartment afterward).

Some of her things are family heirlooms and valuable antiques, and I will discuss ideas about handling those items in Chapter 12. Most of what I'm holding onto, though, isn't valuable to anyone except Dale and me and our memories.

Our formal living room set (which was part of our "J.C. Penney Showroom" as Dale jokingly called our house), our queen sleeper sofa, washer and dryer, my mom's dining room set, and assorted beds will be donated. I plan to find a domestic violence shelter or animal shelter thrift shop for these items. Our goal is to have the "storage building" cleaned out so we can use it to store only what is part of our lives today.

My guess, though, is that most of the items in boxes will get thrown out, which is a testament to how little we really *need*. Living in Our Little House for over eight years has proved to us that what we need isn't a whole lot.

♠

If you're like most people and getting rid of stuff is hard for you, there are organizing experts who can help. Janine Adams—a certified professional organizer and owner of Peace of Mind Organizing in St. Louis, Missouri—almost never recommends renting a storage unit to store stuff. "You're really just wasting money on rent for stuff, most of which never comes out of storage," she says. "It's better to make the decision now rather than after you've paid a lot of money for rental and moving later." She recommends going through belongings once, and then doing it again. If you know you need to eliminate more stuff and can't do it, hire a professional organizer; this is what they're paid to do.

A lot of people who are downsizing to a tiny home have even described getting rid of stuff as "painful." But once they get used to their new little home, they don't miss the possessions they've sold, donated, or given to friends and family.

Sue Smith Moak, who lives in her 464-square-foot cabin in the Texas Hill Country, moved 13 times throughout the course of her marriage with Rick. "With moving a lot, we did get rid of things with each move, but it's amazing how much clutter we still had. Now I have only the things I love and use," Sue says. "I feel like I have taken the scissors to my life and cut out all of the unnecessary parts."

Our commitment to living a clutter-free life in Our Little House is tested daily. I try to live by the "one in, one out" rule. If I purchase a piece of clothing, for example, another piece of clothing has to go. It might not hit the door immediately, but it will during the next rotation of the closet, which happens twice a year in conjunction with the major change of the seasons.

I make it a rule to take stock of the pantry before going grocery shopping. I have a lot of pantry space considering we live in a little home, but we still cannot stock up for months at a time.

In a little home, even a few pieces of paper or junk mail piled on the kitchen table can make the whole house look messy. When we lived in the split-level, we would bring in the mail and either leave it on the stairs to be picked up later or pile it on the kitchen table. A pile of mail on the kitchen table might appear a little messy, but the whole room doesn't get *cluttered* by a few pieces of paper.

Home is a 40-foot catamaran for Diane Selkirk, her husband, Evan Gatehouse, their daughter, Maia—and the family cat, Charlie.

Diane Selkirk lives on a 40-foot catamaran with her husband, Evan Gatehouse, 13-year-old daughter, Maia Selkirk, and a 7-year-old feline named Charlie. The family sails the world in this unusual type of tiny home. But increasingly, people are embracing a variety of small-living options as they choose to live their dreams on their own terms rather than be bound by societal norms.

Diane and Evan have always loved sailing and bought their first boat in 1994. "Evan grew up sailing with his parents, and I went to sailing camps as a kid," Diane says. "We met at sailing instructor school, and we both loved the idea of living aboard and sailing around the world." The couple took some time off from sailing after Maia was born, but hit the seas again when she was seven.

The family has experienced a lot of high adventure and smooth sailing, but when it comes to clutter, they've hit some waves, just like anyone in a little home. With both adults working from their floating tiny home and Maia doing her homeschooling as-signments, things can get messy pretty quickly.

"Things that wouldn't look messy in a large house make a small one look cluttered," Diane says. "Our living room is also the dining, family, and work room. A few books, papers, dishes, and cat toys make it very crowded very quickly."

The dining table also doubles as a desk and a play area.

I personally know that paper-clutter battle very well. I've tried to eliminate excess paper clutter by removing myself from mailing lists for credit offers, catalogs, and other junk mail we don't need. We also found an old-fashioned mailbox at a thrift store for $5. We brought it home, painted it, and hung it on the railing at the writer's studio so Dale can drop the mail there on his way down the driveway in the evening. Since I do all of the paperwork from the studio, it allows me to deal with a bill or shred a piece of junk mail without it ever making it into Our Little House.

Ramona and Carlo DeAngelus live with their dogs—Leroy, Vito (pictured), and Leo—in a 200-square-foot tiny home near Asheville, North Carolina.

Ramona DeAngelus, author of My Amazing Epic Life on Facebook, lives in a 200-square-foot home on seven acres near Asheville, North Carolina, with her husband, Carlo, and she had a similar idea for her mail. "When I check the mail, I put the junk mail into the side panel of my car and take it to work to shred," Ramona says. "Junk mail never even makes it into the house. The bills go in the designated bill slot" in the house.

Before moving to their tiny home, Carlo had a 2,200-square-foot home, and Ramona lived in a 1,500-square-foot home. They purchased their property, which came with a bonus—a 1974 camper—in 2012.

"We donated truckloads full of stuff," says Ramona. "Even now, I can see ways of getting rid of some things."

The couple originally planned to move into the camper and live there full-time, but they quickly realized that it wasn't a sustainable option for them. Campers aren't designed for full-time living, especially in the winter. So, they ditched the camper and built their tiny house on a trailer.

They have adapted to life in their tiny home, but Ramona says of clutter, "I am constantly picking up things."

That constant picking up has led Dale and me to adopt the motto, "a place for everything and everything in its place." Last winter was especially cold and harsh. Dale and I were sick multiple times, and we both had a busy work schedule. We really didn't physically feel good enough to make sure everything was put back where it was supposed to go. By the time the early days of spring came around, our kitchen table was full of junk, and our kitchen counters were overflowing with bottles of spices, the toaster, and other assorted things that needed to be put away.

After we spent an entire weekend cleaning and organizing the cabinets and laundry pantry, Our Little House seemed to release the negative energy we had accumulated over the winter. It felt lighter and brighter. Amazingly, after we got the organizing and cleaning done, neither of us got sick again that season!

Once Our Little House was back in order, we resumed our routine of being able to clean it from top to bottom in about an hour—one of the big advantages of having a small space.

🏠

Like many families, we also face the challenges of what to do with our kids' stuff—the only difference is that our "kids" don't have two legs, but four. We have a dedicated plastic bin in the kitchen for their dog food. When we have guests for dinner, we set it out on the covered front porch. At the split-level, we kept the dog toys in a large crate in the family room. At Our Little House, we just don't buy as many toys (really, how many toys or bones can a dog play with or chew on at once?), and their small collection of toys, ropes, and bones is put in a corner between the television and the futon.

Human kids could present a bigger challenge, however, especially given the materialistic society in which we live today. The Berzinses, who lived with their two children in the 336-square-foot home in Virginia, explain that it wasn't much of an issue for them. The family had been preparing to downsize for quite some time and went through two rounds of purging their things to decide what to keep. "When it came to toys and stuff for their rooms, we gave them each a milk crate and told them that's how much stuff they can have," says Hari. "They both loved stuffed animals, which turned out to be a good thing because they can have them all over their loft." Hari's kids have also developed a love for tiny dollhouse-size figurines. Mostly, though, Hari says her kids are outside "being kids," playing, using their imaginations, building forts, and gathering crawdads and insects in jars.

The Berzins kids' loft doubled the square footage of their tiny home from 168 square feet to 336 square feet.

The Gawtrys—who live in a 728-square-foot home with their twin 7-year-old daughters, Evelyn and Nora—are glad their children are growing up in a little home. "They haven't developed a ridiculous attachment to stuff," says Bec. "Their lives are more about the experiences. They don't get a lot of toys for gifts, but they'll get tickets to a play, for example."

Bunk beds—like these belonging to Evelyn and Nora Gawtry—are a great space-saver in little homes, while a desk built into the wall is just the right size for a computer.

Another place where clutter can gather quickly is in the closet. I love clothes; I always have. When I turned 14, it was those all-important designer jeans that made me want to get a job so I could stop wearing the department store brands my mom bought for me.

When Dale and I began dating, he worked nights at the meat company, and he would sometimes go shopping for me on payday. My mom would allow him to go up to my bedroom, where he would lay out a new outfit that he'd purchased for me on my bed as a surprise for when I got home from school. We lived in the Wilson House at that time, so closet space wasn't a problem. I had one closet in the bedroom and a large cedar closet in my bathroom. In our split-level, there were closets in our bedroom, my office, and in the spare bedroom. We also had a hallway coat closet and a linen closet for extra sheets and towels.

When we moved to Our Little House, I already had a whole set of warm-weather clothing here. (I didn't like packing and lugging clothes back and forth every other weekend.) That meant that after we moved, I simply had to donate more. When you are limited to one five-foot closet for two people, you learn to keep only what you love.

We lived in Our Little House for six years before I felt the need to go out and buy some more fashionable clothes, mainly for professional conferences and meetings. The "one in, one out" rule applies to the whole house—including closets—which means that if I have only what I love in my closet, I have to love the new item much more to make room for it.

All of this makes us conscientious buyers. Nothing can be purchased on a whim.

## Keeping Items for Decorating

When I took what was then called home economics in high school, it became pretty obvious that I wasn't going to win any awards for cooking, sewing, or decorating a home. The pillow I made in sewing didn't resemble a pillow at all. The food I made in cooking class wasn't edible. Worst of all was the grade I got for decorating my fake home.

The teacher wrote on my printed layout that my decor and colors didn't "flow," and made no sense.

My decorating improved a little when we bought our split-level. My formal living room opened to the kitchen. We removed a horrible wallpaper from the tall entryway and painted it (along with the living room and hallway) a white that had a subtle hint of light blue. The living room and kitchen featured country decor, with pink gingham–checked wallpaper in the kitchen (which was there when we purchased the house). But that's where the decor "flow" ended. Our master bathroom was decorated in cats—on the walls, in statues and even the toilet paper holder was a cat. The bedroom was in a nautical theme, and our family room emphasized Native American art.

In a little house, one single theme throughout works best. Our Little House is decorated in natural greens and browns, with splashes of red for color. The running theme is black bears, which is represented on lamps, in the art, and on towels and the valances.

A few of the bear-themed items in our house.

In the living room at the split-level, I displayed a doll collection I'd had since I was a child. It consisted mainly of Victorian era–dressed dolls in what was once an antique pie safe. In the bedroom, I collected seashell jewelry boxes and little wooden lighthouses that sat on our dressers.

In Our Little House, we don't have room for bear-themed knickknacks; our bears serve a purpose like the bear toilet-paper holder and bear soap holder in our bathroom and the two bear lamps and bear pillows in the living room. We have a trash can with bears on it, and even the night-lights feature bears. Every decorative item in our house, except for those on the walls, has a distinct functional purpose.

Houseplants are the exception. While they don't serve a specific function, a house doesn't feel like a home to me without at least a few houseplants. I have a very large Saddle Leaf Philodendron that my mother in-law gave me as a wedding shower gift in 1986. It was a small plant at the time, and I didn't have much of a green thumb, so I didn't plan on having it for long. We were living in our first duplex at the time, and the house was devoid of plants. I saw our marriage as a new beginning for us, the start of our "official" adult lives. My parents didn't have a perfect marriage, but they married after having dated for only six weeks and lasted for 36 years, until death did they part. My mom instilled in me the knowledge that a successful marriage takes lots of love, patience, and nurturing.

Dale caught between Dakota and The Plant.

For the past 30 years, I have given the plant a lot of the same. Like Dale and me, the plant has grown. It went from being in a small pot to a medium one, to a larger medium one. The last time it was transplanted was about 15 years ago into a huge pot that is more likely to be found in the sprawling lobby of an office building than in a home. It was large even for the living room in the split-level.

When we moved to Our Little House, Dale said, "We aren't taking The Plant, are we?" He has long hated it because of its size, and it became known simply as "The Plant." I knew I could likely find a new home for it with one of my McMansion-owning friends, or I could have donated it to a hospital or office building. But I couldn't bear to part with it. The Plant, which had survived my lack of growing skills, had become a representation of the longevity of our marriage. The Plant, like our marriage, has had some ups and downs over the years. It's grown and thrived, and every once in a while, it seems droopy and loses a few leaves. But it always bounces back.

It is, at its roots, solid.

Dale had to move it with a dolly. It spent the first winter with us in Our Little House, blocking the front door from use that season. I have a photo of Dale leaning back in his

The Plant on the Party Deck.

recliner, being playfully attacked from the front by Dakota, who's lying on his chest, and "attacked" from behind by the wild leaves of The Plant.

The Plant, along with a pretty-good-size peace lily that our good friends Mike and Charlotte sent to Mom's funeral, and some of my mom's smaller plants, were eventually moved to the Belle Writer's Studio, where they spend the winter. In the summer, they're moved to the Party Deck. The Plant, like us, really loves it there.

Some of the many signs around Our Little House and the Belle Writer's Studio.

Signs also became a part of the decor in Our Little House. The first one I hung is a wooden sign that points out the back door, exclaiming, "Campfire tonight. Ghost stories told." Another of my favorite signs hangs directly across from where I sit on the futon. It reminds me that, indeed, "Life Is Good."

I've done the same in the Belle Writer's Studio. A rustic wooden sign features a bear that advertises the Ozarks: "Scenic drives with bear jams along the way." Another in the bathroom has a bear in a claw-foot tub advertising baths at the "Lazy Bear Lodge" for 5 cents.

Yet another sign points guests toward the lake. But my two favorites are a wooden sign my mother painted that represents all of the major holidays and says "Happy Everything," and one in the studio that says, "What happens at the cabin, stays at the cabin." The signs are fun and whimsical, and, I think, a good representation of our life.

## Storage

We aren't—nor will we ever be—minimalists. I think it's wonderful if someone can live with a mere one hundred possessions and wants to commit his or her life to that. But for us, it's simply not realistic.

We've taken some criticism from some who perceive the tiny house movement to be about strict minimalism. They didn't believe we were "true" small house dwellers because we have the Belle Writer's Studio and outbuildings in which to store stuff.

I can debate the first point by responding that people who work outside of their home go to an office, and most people who work from home have a room dedicated for office space. I tried working from Our Little House, and it didn't work for me. I wasn't happy.

On the second point, we live in a rural area, and just as it did with our ancestors, rural living requires a certain amount of equipment. We need not only mowers, a trailer, a wood splitter, and equipment to maintain the land, but also vehicles to get to work and to town. Part of living for us is also having recreational toys, such as our boat and ATV. All these need protection from varmints like wood rats, which will eat wires and nest in motors.

In addition, we store extra equipment, such as our cast-iron cookware and lawn furniture, in our garage in the off-season. Even when we rid our lives of the unnecessary stuff that we brought from the city, we still need these outbuildings to store the necessary.

So don't let people make you feel guilty if you don't fit their definition of a minimalist. Don't think you are "not true to the movement" if you have outbuilding storage.

Our outbuilding houses all the equipment necessary to maintain Our Little House.

Jay Shafer paraphrases Shakespeare by saying, the only person you need to be true to is yourself. Living Large looks different for every single one of us.

Although we don't have a lot of space in Our Little House, we had the foresight to design two deep closets (one pantry in the living/kitchen space and one in our bedroom) where we can store shoes and folded clothes. Our bedroom closet is even deep enough to allow for storage of plastic bins containing off-season clothes.

However, many tiny homes don't have that luxury. Ramona and Carlo DeAngelus, who live near Asheville, North Carolina, didn't incorporate any closet space into the design of their tiny home. They decided against having them take up space in their home and planned to store clothes in a separate building. "We brought with us a storage shed where we put our clothes, dresser, and our washer and dryer," says Ramona. While they do have to go outside to access the other building, it is mere steps from their tiny home, so Ramona finds it isn't a problem.

"We really don't mind the arrangement, it gives us more room for actual living instead of closet space in our tiny home," she says.

Clever storage solutions that make living in a small space comfortable include storage under a seat (top left), as seen here in the Courains' window seat, or under the stairs, where Ariel McGlothin has installed drawers (top right) and the Howes have put a washer and dryer (bottom left). Tammy Strobel even has extra storage under her refrigerator (bottom right).

The key to Living Large is having enough stuff to live and be happy, but not so much that it is cluttering your life.

## LIVING LARGE TIPS:
### Design (or Even Retrofit) Some Storage
### into Your Little Home

- Think of every piece of furniture as having potential for hidden storage. Our end tables have built-in lamps and magazine racks. If you need a side or coffee table, make sure you choose one that will also open to offer additional storage, such as the one the Courains use as their window seat. Ariel McGlothin designed her built-in corner couches and her stairs to have storage compartments.

- Make use of every bit of dead space that you can. Sue Smith Moak stores belongings in plastic containers under her bed. The Howes designed their home so that the space underneath the stairs served as a laundry closet for their washer and dryer.

- Choose furniture and accessories that can do double-duty. In both Our Little House and the Belle Writer's Studio, we have two futons that are couches by day and guest beds when needed.

- For some reason, little house dwellers typically have another thing in common: We love our books. If you're building a new home, try to incorporate built-in bookshelves. If you still don't have enough room, keep only the important books that you love. For me, that included a lot of my mom's books, some of which were the first books I read as a child. Sue Smith Moak transferred most of the books that wouldn't fit in their bunkhouse to an e-reader. "I like hardcover books for reference or local interest and history books," Sue says.

# 7

# Party on the Deck:
## Making the Outdoors
## an Extension of Your Little House

*Living Truth: In the spring, I'm ready for warm, sunny days on the porch with a tall glass of iced coffee. By fall, I'm ready for crisp mornings on the porch with a steaming mug of hot coffee and a cozy blanket.*

One Saturday night last summer—on one of those rare nights in this part of the country when the humidity was low—I sat on our Party Deck at dusk.

The deck is so named because it's been the scene of many a happy gathering at Our Little House. Outdoor spaces are very important to tiny house dwellers. They allow us to entertain in good weather and can keep us from getting cabin fever in bad weather.

When we finished Our Little House in 2003, we invited everyone we knew (all of about six people at the time) down for a barbecue on the deck. Since then, we've invited friends from Kansas City for dinners, as well as other neighbors. When friends and family visit, the deck is the gathering spot. If it's hot, we hook up one of our large fans and put up the table umbrella. After a few cold drinks, no one seems to notice the heat.

On this summer night, however, it was just me and the dogs and the woodland critters. The dogs were lying lazily, and I had come outside to join them, escaping noise of the television show Dale was watching. I had my music playlist going, and the song "Dixieland Delight" by Alabama came on. How appropriate, I thought. This wasn't Tennessee, but

I could hear a croaking bullfrog down in our hollow and a deer snorting in the distance.

I turned off the music and let the woods serenade the dogs and me. I listened to "our" owl, the one we hear most of the year, calling to its mate. I watched the last humming-birds of the day come to the feeder to get a little nibble before settling in for the night.

As dusk grew deeper, lightning bugs entertained me with their blinking, and the coy-otes began their mournful howls in the distance. When night finally fell and I looked up and saw all the bright stars—heavenly lights that city dwellers usually cannot experi-ence due to light pollution—I was surprised to realize I had been sitting there, in the moment, for *two full hours*.

Dale and I and all our plants love the Party Deck.

I love our Party Deck. At 12 by 24 feet, running the full length of the back of the house, it adds more than 50 percent of additional space to Our Little House. Our split-level in Kansas City also had a deck, but it wasn't large enough to entertain a crowd.

I knew from the beginning that I wanted our deck to be large enough to entertain. We originally planned for the deck to encircle the entire house, but we ran out of con-struction funds and had to downsize our plan. Nonetheless, the Party Deck can accommodate a small crowd and is also large enough to host all of my houseplants (including The Plant) and a container garden in the summer.

Sometimes, when the mosquitoes become overwhelming, which they often do thanks to the lake behind our house, we wish we had covered and screened the deck. However, on sunny days, when I walk home from the air-conditioned studio, I often sit on the Party Deck to soak in some vitamin D and warm my bones. I don't think I would want the Party Deck any other way.

Plus, for days when we don't want to soak up the sun, or if we want to sit and watch the rain fall, we have the covered front porch. One weekend, when the house was nearing completion, we came down to check on the progress. A summer storm rolled in while we were inspecting the work that had been done that week.

Dale and I went out onto the covered front porch, which didn't yet have railings, and sat on the edge, dangling our feet and listening to the rain on the roof. Although the rain wasn't actually hitting us, it seemed to wash away the stress that two months of long-distance home construction had levied on us. From that moment, I knew that I would always love this space and it would be my peaceful retreat.

In 2005, when I was finishing writing a book about my brother Steve (about his experiences in Vietnam and the alcoholism I now believe was due to post-traumatic stress disorder), I retreated to the covered front porch to work. It was another one of those rare July days in which the humidity had given us temporary reprieve. We were at Our Little House for a vacation, but we had work to do around the homestead. Dale was working in the garage, and I had to do a final edit of the manuscript before it was published. The story, which ended with my brother's death from alcohol poisoning at age 47, was cathartic, but also difficult to write.

Hershey, our beloved dachshund, was also in the end stages of kidney disease and was lying in her bed by my feet. Hershey was on a lot of medication, most of which made her sleep, but she loved being outside. Even in a drug-induced haze, she was always aware if I wasn't nearby. The porch brought us both some comfort on that summer day.

The covered front porch is where I most strongly feel the presence of the people and animals I love but are no longer with me. During that reading, I felt Steve's presence. I now have one of my mom's favorite antiques, an ice-cream table set with a marble top and chairs, on that porch. In favorable weather, I sit out there in the mornings and drink my coffee. Next to the ice-cream set is the antique lantern my dad used to carry at the railroad. The graves of Hershey and our red dachshund, Molly, are side by side in the woods, just beyond but visible from the porch.

The covered front porch, with my mom's ice-cream table set and my dad's lantern at the far end; the view from the porch.

When the wind chimes play their soft music, it is a place where I can feel all of their spirits.

Everything has its pros and cons. The pro of living and working in paradise, as I have the opportunity to do, is that *I'm living and working in paradise*. The con is that I still have to work. Although I love what I do, on beautiful spring, summer, and fall days, there is nothing I'd rather be doing than enjoying the outdoors.

There may not be an app for that, but fortunately there is a deck for that.

The covered front porch on the Belle Writer's Studio serves as our third outdoor space. This porch allows me to unhook my laptop on beautiful days and write outside without the sun beating down or blinding my view of the computer screen. It also allows our guests, when they visit, to sit outside and enjoy a nice cup of coffee before the day's adventures get into full swing.

The porch on the Belle Writer's Studio.

Our final outdoor space is our fire pit. A rural house wouldn't be a true home without an outdoor fire pit. We hope to someday build a full-scale outdoor kitchen with a patio and outdoor fireplace. But for now, around the fire pit is a good place to sit back, relax, and chat with friends. As I mentioned before, the little wooden sign on the wall next to the back door of Our Little House directs everyone with an arrow that reads, "Campfire tonight. Ghost stories told."

When I was going through stuff at the split-level before the big move to Our Little House, I ran across a letter I had written to Dale when I was a teenager on vacation with my parents at the Lake of the Ozarks. My friend Lora had come with us on that trip, and as I read the letter, I thought about Lora and me going down to our dock at night and floating in the lake on inner tubes. We giggled and told stories and looked up at the stars, wondering what our futures would hold.

After reading the letter, I had a strong urge to find out what happened to Lora and our other friend, Shelly. As happens so often with school pals, I had lost touch. I found Lora through social media, and she knew how to reach Shelly. In 2009, the three of us decided to get together for a reunion "slumber party weekend" at Our Little House.

Sometime after we added The Belle Writer's Studio and the second outbuilding, Dale and I dubbed our property "Campbell Town." As we enter the driveway, our property does resemble a town of sorts, with the storage building on one side, the Belle Writer's Studio on another, and then Our Little House and the garage at the end of the driveway.

Together, Our Little House, the Belle Writer's Studio, the garage, and the outbuilding (not pictured) make up Campbell Town.

When Lora and Shelly arrived at Campbell Town, we didn't go down to the lake and float on inner tubes at night. (We now know there are snakes in those lakes. Yikes!) But Dale did build us a fire in the fire pit so we could sit around that Saturday night, enjoying our first drinks together as legal adults. We didn't tell ghost stories—well, maybe, if you count talking about old times. Some of those recollections of teenage shenanigans are

scary enough to be ghost stories! But it was a nice atmosphere in which to sit and remi-
nisce. Our slumber party weekends are now an annual affair, held in different places, but
we'll never forget that first one at Campbell Town and being around the fire that night.

🏠

Outdoor living is important to most small home dwellers, including Connie Howe and
her husband, Ken. When they decided to build their park model home near Olympia,
Washington, they made sure to design a beautiful outdoor space.

The indoor/outdoor fireplace makes the Howes' deck an ideal place to entertain.

When the Howes designed their home, they included a double indoor/outdoor fireplace in the living room. One side is accessible from the living room, while the other
faces the outdoors, so they can sit on their deck and enjoy a cozy fire on a crisp night.

The couple also built a very attractive outdoor kitchen and bar, where they love to entertain guests. "Summers here are beautiful and great for outdoor living," says Connie. "We've become the party house of the neighborhood."

🏠

Outdoor living doesn't only mean having decks and outdoor kitchens, though. Kevin Kalley installed an outdoor shower off of the lanai next to his small Hawaiian house, which is common for many homes in warm tropical climates.

Talk about a tub with a view! When Ramona and Carlo DeAngelus couldn't fit a bathtub in their 200-square-foot home, they decided to put one outside.

And for tiny house dwellers who prefer baths rather than showers, even outdoor bathtubs are possible. The 200-square-foot home of Ramona DeAngelus in North Carolina has only a shower, but that didn't stop her from yearning for a tub. "We just got an outside bathtub, and that space is currently a work in progress," Ramona says. "It will be enclosed, and we're putting in black stone. It has Jacuzzi jets, and we call it our 'redneck tub.' In the summer, we will be able to take bubble baths under the stars."

The couple even built an awesome outdoor space for their large dog, Vito, whom they rescued as a stray. "He showed up and never left," says Ramona. "We're outside with him all the time, but he can't come into the house at night—he's too big, and his tail just knocks everything over."

Carlo built Vito his very own bunker underneath the storage shed next to the house. "He even put a woodstove down there for him. We didn't want him to be cold in the winter," Ramona says. "We spent half the summer stacking firewood for the dog."

---

**LIVING LARGE TIPS:** Building Great Outdoor Spaces

---

- Devote a significant building budget to your outdoor spaces. They are very important for little house living.

- When designing an outdoor kitchen, you don't have to have it all. For example, if you don't think you will use a pizza oven, which are popular in outdoor kitchens, don't include that expense. Create only the space you will use.

- Decide how much room you will need to entertain, and make your patio or deck a few feet larger.

# 8

# We Only Have One Planet:
## Living a More Sustainable Life

*Living Truth:* We have a clothes dryer, but why use it when the wind
and the sun give us a true fresh scent?

Growing up in the 1970s made me environmentally aware. The first Earth Day was celebrated in 1970, and the "Keep America Beautiful" advertisements against littering were frequently shown on television. The most memorable of those ads featured a Native American shedding a tear over what we were doing to our beautiful country. That image made a very powerful impression on me.

In 1988, my mom and I saw some cloth bags for sale in the grocery store. We decided it would be a great way to help the environment while simultaneously reducing the clutter of plastic bags in our homes. By doing our shopping together, we were able to remind each other to bring our bags. It was a little difficult at first, but after a few months, remembering the bags became automatic.

Dale, who worked for the largest landfill in our area, was overwhelmed by the trash he saw arriving on a daily basis. He would shake his head and say, "Saving a few bags a week isn't going to help anything." In the 1980s, not many shoppers in the Midwest were carrying cloth bags. Young gum-chewing checkers and pimple-faced sackers looked at us like we were from Mars when we handed them a wad of cloth bags (and sometimes they still do). Mom used her bags until she passed away in 2007, and now I have all of them and use them to this day.

When I brought the bags to Our Little House and continued using them, Dale still rolled his eyes. By then, we'd had those bags for 20 years. I estimated that in that time, Mom and I combined had saved at least 15,000 plastic bags from the landfill. I think even Dale was impressed when I showed him the number. A dozen bags in a week may not make much of a difference, but over time, it all adds up. Not using them also helps save the clutter of the plastic at Our Little House.

So I wasn't new to environmental awareness when we moved to Our Little House, and I was very pleased that having a smaller home would lessen our carbon footprint on the environment.

According to the "CoolClimate" calculator tool sponsored by the University of California, Berkley, the average two-person household in our income bracket in our region emits a total of 46.2 tons of carbon dioxide emissions each year.[23] The calculator determines a home's carbon footprint by adding up what a family uses in categories such as housing, food, and transportation. In the category of housing—which is based on a 1,850-square-foot home that uses electricity, natural gas, and other fuel—the average is 116 tons. I calculated our carbon emission using 800 square feet (Our Little House and the Belle Writer's Studio combined), and we emit only 8.2 tons. This is likely even smaller since I input an "average" calculation of electricity usage, and we probably aren't in the average range. I hang most of our laundry outdoors, and we heat Our Little House with a woodstove.

Dale and I also reduce our carbon footprint in the category of food, thanks to my having switched to a 90-percent vegan diet in 2013. Using the calculator, I learned that we emit 4.9 tons of food-related carbon dioxide versus 5.6 tons on average. A plant-based diet—full of beans, grains, vegetables, and fruit—leaves a smaller carbon imprint than consuming meat. In the category of shopping, we also save. Having a little home doesn't allow us to go to a warehouse store and stock up on items anymore, so we don't purchase things we really don't need or use before it expires. The manufacture of new furniture, clothing, etc., emits carbon emissions. By buying less, we're consuming fewer items, and that helps us save in our emissions. Our estimated emission in the shopping category is 5.8 tons of carbon dioxide, versus the average of 10.9. Even in the category of travel, which I thought might be more than average, we are emitting 15.9 tons versus the average of 18.1. This is most likely due to the fact that if I need something to cook for dinner, I typically call Dale at work, and he picks it up while he is in town. Except for trips for business, I drive very little. Our grocery and errand trips are usually always together.

In total, the calculator shows that we emit about 34.7 tons of carbon dioxide per year, versus the average of 46.2 tons. I would still like to improve upon that, and at the end of the calculator, there's a place where I made several pledges to make that score come down next year.

♠

Living closer to nature makes us want to be better environmentalists. We no longer use chlorine bleach or harsh chemicals, especially in the drains or anywhere they could leech into the ground, which could poison our well water. As the saying goes, only stupid people would poison their own well. Pesticides and herbicides are also out. I didn't use them in the city either, because I was aware that the runoff enters the storm drain system and eventually finds its way into the city's water supply.

However, for many in the city and suburbs, it's easier to pretend poisons and trash don't directly affect us. For many folks, it's tempting to not pay attention to trash and paper and what happens to it when we throw it out. When you have a septic system, though, you can't even pretend it gets flushed away. It goes into a huge concrete container in your yard, where the solids are composted so the broken-down waste can flow out into a leech field underground. Harsh chemicals like bleach can kill the bacteria that are necessary to break down the solids—and this isn't good. If the bacteria doesn't break down the solids, it could cause a system backup. Additionally, a lot of toilet paper can clog a septic system, which could cause it to back up into your house. Think of the movie *Meet the Parents*, when the septic backs up into the yard—it could be a disaster.

In the country, we don't have trash pickup. We have to haul it to the county's transfer station ourselves, which makes us much more aware of the trash we're producing. I try to buy things with minimal packaging, but it's not always easy. Purchasing bulk items such as rice and beans at the health-food store has helped with this. I also recently bought reusable little cloth bags for the bulk items, which I can take to the store and fill with beans, rice, and other items in just the amount I need.

As for water, which is becoming a premium resource for drought-stricken regions like California, we don't use as much as we did in the city. When we first built Our Little House and had our water delivered—before we dug our well—we quickly learned to conserve. I don't run water the whole time I'm brushing my teeth or washing my face. I make sure I have a full load of laundry before washing clothes. I also don't rinse dishes in running water. Instead, I use a trick I learned when camping: putting rinse water in a square plastic tub.

One thing that I love about the Berzins family in rural Virginia is that their children are learning these lessons early, as our ancestors did. They are aware of the seasons and what plants should be blooming when, and they take note of the creek freezing in the winter months.

Sue Smith Moak, who lives on her rural Texas property, has found that being close to nature can be healing as well. After her husband, Rick, passed away in the late fall of 2014, Sue questioned whether she should have moved to their little cabin without him and spent the last years of his life largely apart. Sue retired before Rick and went ahead and moved to their rural property while he stayed in Houston for work. When all of the plants—some of which they had planted together—began to bloom the following spring, the theme of renewal overwhelmed her.

Sue Smith Moak's late husband Rick, cooking up a storm in their outdoor kitchen.

Sue realized they had planted the seeds of a good life on their rural property, and she came to the conclusion that she may not have had the courage to move after Rick's death and be completely on her own. Sue became grateful for having had the chance to learn how to live in the natural surroundings part-time while Rick was alive so she would be prepared to do it full-time after he was gone.

Ariel McGlothin, who lives in her off-grid cabin in the mountains near Jackson, Wyoming, says she isn't especially interested in environmentalism, but by living in a tiny house, it simply comes with the lifestyle. "I'm more into independence, which being off-grid gives me," says Ariel. She taps into her neighbor's water well, with their permission, and uses about 140 gallons per month. According to a report by the U.S. Geological Survey, the average American uses between 80 and 100 gallons of water *per day*.[24]

When Dale and I are out enjoying nature, we see more clearly that we are all indeed related and that each part of the natural order connects to the next. When I see the remnants of a burst balloon, its string still tied to it, lying in the road, I pick it up. It may be a symbol of remembrance or celebration for those who launched it, but what goes up must come down. This trash can be potentially harmful to birds or other wildlife. Rural dwellers know these animals—we watch them play and eat; we hear them sing; and we protect the nests on our property from our dogs and other predators. These creatures are our neighbors, and this is *our* neighborhood. There is a delicate balance out here in our woods.

In 2010, we learned a very difficult lesson of the consequences that can happen when that precarious balance is suddenly shifted. A mountain lion had long been spotted by locals at the top of our mountain. Almost everyone who'd lived here for any length of time had a story of either hearing or seeing it.

That summer, a land developer looking to make a small fortune, started clear-cutting the top of the mountain. We heard that his plan was to sell the land in five-acre lots with a "lake view" (never mind that the lake was miles away).

One night in June, I awoke to a horrible screeching sound, which can only be described as sounding like a woman in terrible distress. I had heard this noise once before and was told by locals that it was a mountain lion on the attack. Oddly, Emma, our German shepherd/rottweiler mix, was the only dog that woke to it as well. She frantically barked as the screaming continued for several minutes.

On August 9, after a long hot spell, Emma, Sade (our pit bull), and Chloe (a black lab mix) wanted to go outside before we went to bed. We didn't usually let them out at night, but the dogs were restless, as they'd been cooped up during the heat of the day. Dale and I decided to let them go outside.

What could go wrong with three dogs together protecting each other? At about 3:30 a.m., I awoke to that same shriek, only I could have sworn a dog's yip preceded it. "Emma," I mumbled in a sleepy voice. My eyes opened, and I listened for any other sounds, but there were none. No shrieking, no yelping, no barking from any of the dogs. Our two small dogs, Dakota and Molly, had not awakened. I was very tired and convinced myself that it must have been a dream.

When we got up that morning, Sade and Chloe were on the porch. They bolted into the house as soon as we opened the door. "Emma?" I called, but there was no response. I immediately remembered my experience about an hour before. I called for her frantically and took the flashlight to look for her under the porch. I told Dale what happened, and he searched before leaving for work. "She'll turn up," he said. "She's probably just chasing a rabbit." But I knew better. Emma never wandered off without the other dogs, and Sade and Chloe had been terrified when I let them in the door.

Kerri holding Emma, with Molly in the foreground, shortly after building Our Little House in 2003.

We walked those woods for six weeks, searching in dense poison ivy and oak and trying to avoid snakes. We followed buzzards circling in the sky. My heart breaks every time we lose one of our fur kids, but it's harder losing them when you never know what really happened.

We continued the search for her remains after the leaves fell, but we never found a trace of our beloved dog, not even her collar. We went from hope of finding her alive to only hoping for discovering her remains so we could bury her. All my dogs are special, but Emma was a very special dog, having saved me from getting stomped by one of our horses just six months after we took her in. I felt I had failed to protect her as she had me.

Despite their frightening experience, Chloe (top) and Sade (bottom) still enjoy the outdoors.

I second-guessed our decision to let them out that night. I will always regret not getting up and waking Dale immediately when I heard those sounds that fateful morning.

It wasn't until I was telling a neighbor who lived at the top of the mountain about the incident that she told me of another neighbor who had lost two large Great Pyrenees dogs in broad daylight on the same day. Just like the incident with Emma, the neighbor heard shrieks but found nothing left of her dogs. "Maybe its better you didn't get up that morning," my friend said. "I hear when they strike, it's already too late. There's probably nothing you could have done for her, and you might have gotten hurt trying."

My last image of Emma will always be her trotting up the driveway into the darkness, her tail wagging as she playfully ran with Chloe and Sade.

My aunt suggested that the clear-cutting at the top of the mountain had probably dislocated the big cat and driven it down to our hollow. Local hunters, who told me that there are big cats in these woods, agreed it's likely that this is what happened to Emma, as they can carry off large prey without leaving a trace. Bears, the hunters told me, typically will not attack, and if they did, I would have heard a more prolonged fight, and we likely would have found Emma's body.

We had lost our Cali cat in the first few weeks we lived here, but never thought anything big enough to take down a ninety-pound dog would come that close to our house—and it might not have if the cat's home at the top of the mountain hadn't been destroyed. Since that night, we take our place here in these woods more seriously. We intentionally don't let the dogs out at night, though Chloe and Abbi, who can be quite the hooligans, have escaped by accident. Since August 9, 2010, our once-adventurous Sade, who used to roam with Emma, rarely leaves the deck, even during the day.

We love the fact that we are close to nature and that our little house living helps the environment in big ways. We try to be mindful of everything we do and try not to upset the balance of nature. But we also have to be mindful that we are in the wild.

---

## LIVING LARGE TIPS:
### Helping the Planet—and Helping
### Save Space in a Little Home

---

- Carry cloth bags with you when you go shopping. The production of plastic bags requires the use of fuel and other chemicals. It's estimated that the average American family uses 1,500 bags per year, many of which are not recycled and end up in a landfill.

- Remove your address from catalog and junk-mail lists. This also helps reduce unneeded clutter in your little home. Catalog Choice allows you to manage your catalog subscriptions and will even send notification to companies for you: www.catalogchoice.org. You can get off of junk mail lists by going to www.directmail.com/mail_preference.

- Instead of purchasing plastic bag clips that will end up in the landfill, use wooden clothespins to seal bags of chips and other foods in your pantry.

- If you live in a neighborhood that will allow you to hang your clothes out to dry, do it. Clothes dryers in most other countries are used sparingly. Hanging clothes out to dry saves not only energy, but also money on your utility bill.

- Use environmentally friendly cleaning products.

- Reuse, recycle, and reduce. When planning to buy something, ask yourself if you can purchase it used at an antique or thrift store. It took me months, but I finally came across a full set of Revere Ware that was gently used, didn't contain the chemicals of nonstick cookware, and was made in America. Recycle everything you can and reduce waste (ditch the paper plates!).

- Shop local. Farmers' markets aren't the only place where you can buy locally farmed and raised products. Many cities and small towns have natural-food stores that buy from local farmers. Not buying factory-farmed products laced with pesticides helps the environment *and* your local, small farmer.

- Walk when and where you can. Are you close enough to school to ditch taking your child by car? Can you walk to your grocer?

- Always think about ways you can do better. When we moved here, we couldn't drink the water because it was delivered by truck. Bottled water is a huge problem and should be avoided unless you have a safety concern about your tap water. My next step is eliminating paper towels this year by buying cloth diapers and cutting them up for quick cleaning and counter wipe-ups. Just yesterday, I finally gave up my print newspaper and took the online subscription.

# 9

# Simple Homemade Living:
## Living Large Is Living Healthier and Thriftier

*Living Truth: There's nothing that says "home" like walking into the house on a winter day and being hit with the aroma of a fresh pot of vegetable soup simmering on the stove.*

Some people eat to live, and some people live to eat. You could say that Dale and I fit into the latter category.

When we met, Dale was 18, and I was 15. My exposure to eating out at that time was going with my parents to one of the local steakhouses; one was Bonanza and the other was Ponderosa. We went out to dinner once a month, when my dad got his check from the railroad on the fifteenth of the month. (The check on the first of the month was for the bills.)

I got to choose the restaurant only when it was a special occasion, such as my birthday or if I had gotten a good report card. I always chose Arthur Treacher's Fish and Chips, a fast-food restaurant. I didn't get fish at home because my mom didn't like it. As a child, she was forced to drink cod liver oil every day as a vitamin supplement and said every time she so much as smelled fish, she could taste that nasty cod liver oil and feel the texture in her mouth.

When Dale and I met, our first date was at a McDonald's. Not long after that, he took me to Red Lobster, and I thought I had died and gone to heaven. When we married, we were DINCs (double-income, no children), with quite a bit of discretionary income. Eating out became our hobby, and our tastes evolved beyond chain-restaurant fare. We ate our way through our 20s and 30s at many of Kansas City's best locally owned ethnic restaurants.

We particularly love Mexican food, so when a restaurant opened in the strip mall about six blocks from our house, well, let's just say we were regulars. We could walk down the street and not only indulge in huge portions of food, but also have a few beers without the fear of getting a DUI on the way home.

When we moved to Our Little House, we didn't have the option of walking to the local Mexican cantina or even getting into the car and driving 10 minutes to my favorite sushi bar, as I had done so many nights when Dale was working.

That trip to the sushi bar two or three nights a week became a coping mechanism for me as my mother's health deteriorated. After taking my mom dinner, that I had prepared before Dale left for his night shift, we would sit and visit. I could see almost daily that she was becoming weaker, and it was becoming harder and harder for her to breathe.

A few pieces of sushi, a beer, and sometimes conversation with the chefs or someone sitting next to me at the bar helped me decompress from my daily visits and, for just a little while, made me think of something besides wondering what life would be like without my mother, my best friend. One night, I even met a woman at the sushi bar who became a good friend and was instrumental in helping me after my mom's death.

Using food to cope had become such a habit for me that it made it even harder to transition to rural life. The thing we missed most about city life was the food, especially ethnic fare. The nearest larger town is 50 minutes away, and it offers mostly chain restaurants. The smaller town closer to us has even more limited offerings.

Eventually, I decided that if we were going to continue to eat good food, I would have to learn to cook. During our 21-year marriage, I had, of course, cooked. But I was brought up on mostly processed foods. After raising her older children in the late 1940s and 1950s, and mostly cooking from scratch, Mom thought convenience foods were a miracle.

Oh, she made special dinners on Sundays: pot roast and potatoes, pork chops, meatloaf, chili, and soups. But during the week, when Dad was working his second job and it was the two of us, it was canned spaghetti sauce, chow mein in a can (thank heavens my best friend in junior high introduced me to real Chinese food), and boxed noodles that are supposed to "help" hamburger.

The first recipe I tried at Our Little House required one clove of freshly minced garlic. I only had a bottle of dried minced garlic and had no idea what a clove even was. The next week I bought a garlic bulb and looked on the Internet for the definition of "clove." Then I bought a garlic mincer at a neighbor's in-home kitchen party where women gather, drink wine, and buy items from a salesperson. I was finally on the path to learning my way around a real kitchen.

I also found that by making dinners from semi-scratch—I still used ingredients like canned tomatoes and packaged spaghetti—I was actually saving money. I can buy a jar of prepared spaghetti sauce and have enough for one dinner and maybe one lunch. If I buy three cans of tomato sauce and a can of diced tomatoes and make the sauce adding the spices myself, I have enough for our dinner, two lunches, and typically enough to freeze for one more dinner. It tastes better than jarred sauce, and I've made Dale a fan of my spaghetti.

Our cozy kitchen (top left), with lots of built-in cabinets (top right) and a hidden lazy Susan (bottom left); the view from the kitchen window that I enjoy while washing dishes (bottom right).

Thankfully, when we were building Our Little House, we knew that we wouldn't be jaunting anywhere to eat out, and we built a kitchen equipped with full-size appliances. The exception is the dishwasher. Our only experience with septic systems was knowing relatives who had an old one. Their septic backed up every time the dishwasher ran, so we were a little skittish. We later found out that most septic tanks can handle dishwashers as long as the septic is properly maintained.

Honestly? I'm glad we didn't install one. Back in our split-level, unless we had people over, we only ran our dishwasher when it had a full load, about once a week. We no longer have a set of eight dishes, so if we had a dishwasher, we would have to run it as soon as we used our only four, which would have been wasteful.

We also have a routine in which Dale rinses the dishes off before we go to bed and I wash them in the morning, as the sun is rising. I don't mind because it allows me to watch the wonderful sunrises and hummingbirds at the feeder while standing at the sink. In good weather the window is open, so as a bonus I hear the serenade of the birds, and very often, one of the three types of owls that live in our woods.

We have quite a bit of cabinet space, including a nifty tall baking sheet cabinet and a built-in lazy Susan, which offers lots of space to store pantry items and uses corner space that would otherwise be inaccessible. My top cabinets are recessed from the ceiling, in case I want to use that space for storage. However, I prefer to keep that area clutter-free and use the shelves in my laundry pantry for small appliances and extra utensils.

The challenge is keeping the limited counter space clear of clutter so I have room to chop fresh vegetables and mince that garlic!

🏠

Many people joining the tiny house movement are doing so to either live healthier or more frugally, or with an eye toward helping the environment—or a combination of all those reasons. This can mean mostly cooking at home.

"Cooking is a big deal for me," says Ramona DeAngelus. "I knew that, so I devoted over half of our tiny house to the kitchen." Ramona's husband, Carlos, built custom-made cabinets that suited their needs perfectly. Ramona still needed to eliminate some things, especially multiples. "When we moved here, I did an assessment of what I had and what I needed, and had to be honest with myself. I didn't need 20 mixing bowls."

Ramona kept one large and one small frying pan, baking pans, and just a few other pans. She and Carlos incorporated storage under the fridge and above the cabinets for items such as their Crock-Pot. They hang their coffee cups from hooks. "We have a lot of storage space that is empty, and even now, I can see a way to get rid of more things," says Ramona.

Ramona's husband Carlos custom-built the cabinets in their tidy kitchen.

Cooking is also an important part of Ariel McGlothin's life. Although her home is only 229 square feet, she designed it with a dining-room table that can fold out for guests, a four-burner stove with full-size oven, a small refrigerator with a freezer, and a double-basin sink. Ariel's investment in kitchen real estate has served her well, especially since she barters home-cooked meals for her land rent and gym membership.

Ariel McGlothin's tiny home may be only 229 square feet, but her kitchen has a surprising abundance of storage space.

Ariel's cooking is a combination of dishes she grew up with and ideas of her own creation. She loves to cook with foods that are in season and local. "Due to my own health and the limitations of a few of the folks I cook for, my menus are mostly grain- and dairy-free. Not strictly a primal or paleo diet, but close," she says.

Her dishes include a roast lamb with morel mushrooms, garlic, onions, and carrots, served with a side of greens. She also makes mini elk meat loaves and serves these with gluten-free pasta tossed in pesto and Danish Christmas cabbage. Another mouth-watering dish is citrus and garlic baked chicken wings with broccoli and dairy-free homemade ranch dressing.

Eliminating the unnecessary, particularly in the kitchen, can be painful for some. Happy memories and family celebrations are often centered on food in our culture. I always thought I would someday have my mother's wedding china, which I think was a gift from my grandmother, in my china cabinet. I now don't have room for either the collection or the china cabinet.

I do have a few items—a bowl that belonged to my grandmother and my mom's favorite vinegar carafe—but I still find myself trying to figure out how to use that china in Our Little House. I've thought about using it as our everyday dishes. It is certainly something I love, and I believe things you love should be seen every day. When we break the last of our four regular plates, I will most likely do it.

Sentimental feelings about kitchen items are common. Mary Dunning, who moved into her tiny house after losing her large horse ranch in Missouri during the recession, still feels a pang of sentimentality for certain things she left behind. "Sometimes, when doing a household chore or experimenting with a new recipe, I suddenly need a particular tool or baking dish and then realize it's gone," she says. "That's always a little sad for me. I'm happy with the way things turned out, but the process was painful and I do miss some of my more treasured belongings."

🏠

When I was a kid, my dad planted a vegetable garden every year. My mom especially loved fresh tomatoes, and told us stories of how as a child she would go out to the tomato garden on her grandfather's farm, pick a few, add salt, and eat them while they were still warm from the sun.

Every place I've lived, there has always been a garden where I could pick a fresh tomato and eat it while it was still warm from the vine.

I do a bit of gardening here at Our Little House. We don't have the dark, fertile soil found in Kansas, and we live on the side of a mountain with rocky terrain, so we container garden on the Party Deck. We hope to build raised beds in the future.

I typically plant at least three varieties of tomatoes, tomatillos, various peppers, cilantro, and cucumber. Our little container garden saves us money, and gardening definitely helps the mind and soul. My vegetable containers are interspersed with my annual-flower pots, which brings the Party Deck to life in the summer—or, as Dale likes to say, "makes it full really fast."

Many tiny house enthusiasts I've spoken to also garden. "I put in a sizeable garden and can, dry, and freeze food," says Ariel McGlothin. "I also pickle and ferment my own food."

Some people who live in little homes live almost entirely off of the land. Vicki Salmon lives on five acres outside of Fairbanks, Alaska, with her husband, Willie. When the bottom fell out of oil prices in the 1980s and '90s, cheap gasoline may have been good for the rest of the country, but in oil- and gas-rich areas like Texas and Alaska, it caused a deep recession. "I bought a home with my previous husband, and it took us fifteen years not to be upside down in it," says Vicki. "We couldn't sell it, and we were stuck. I finally sold it in 2000, but I really didn't know how to have a home any other way."

Vicki and Willie had been married seven years when they decided to live in a rustic, off-grid cabin in an area of Alaska that was only accessible by air or boat. They wanted to live debt-free and learn how to live off of the land. When they purchased their current property in 2010, they decided to build only what they could afford and to add on or build their dream home, a log cabin, later. They began with a 12-by-16-foot cabin that they eventually expanded to 500 square feet. When they finished their tiny cabin, they bought the logs for their dream cabin as they could afford them.

Vicki says that they have "severe" cold weather in the winter but that most people don't realize that they also have very nice summers near Fairbanks. They enjoy 70- and 80-degree temperatures, which allow them to enjoy the outdoors and grow their own food.

"We're outside all the time, and we built an awesome outdoor cooking area," says Vicki. "We have a lot of wild berries all through the summer, including blueberries, salmon berries, and low-bush cranberries. I also have a nice big garden, and we have moose, fish, and caribou. We try to be as self-sufficient as possible."

Outside their 500-square-foot home near Fairbanks, Alaska, Vicki and Willie Salmon designed an outdoor cooking and picnic area (top left) and try to live off the land as much as possible by growing an extensive garden (top right). They started with an old-fashioned wall tent with a woodstove (bottom).

Our eating habits in the city resulted in Dale and I truly Living *Large*. We both struggle with weight issues and the health problems that often accompany obesity. In January

2013, I called Dale at work to have him take me to the emergency room—I thought I was having a heart attack. My dad's sudden death at age 58 made me aware that I was at a high risk for diabetes and heart disease, but I hadn't done a lot to avoid it.

After being diagnosed with hypertension and put on a very strong medication to regulate my blood pressure, I resolved to live a healthier life. I adopted a largely vegan diet, eliminating most dairy and meat. I started walking at least a mile a day. In that first year, I lost twenty pounds and was able to get off of the blood-pressure medication.

The biggest challenge to eating a healthy, made-from-semi-scratch diet in a little home is having room in your kitchen for the necessary tools and ingredients. This can be tricky, especially if you don't prepare.

Although I devoted a lot of real estate to the kitchen, we still can't go to the nearest warehouse store and buy gallons of ketchup at a time. But with all the cabinets and the Lazy Susan, we have enough space to store enough food to last two to three weeks. We store appliances we don't use every day, such as the toaster, mixer, Crock-Pot, and food processor, on a shelf in the laundry closet.

Living in Our Little House has taught me so much about experimenting in the kitchen and cooking with different foods and spices. While we still enjoy eating out, some of our most enjoyable times at home now involve the preparation of our meals.

## EXPERT TIPS: Brette Sember

Getting back to the basics of what you actually need in the kitchen can be a daunting task. Brette Sember, author of *The Organized Kitchen,* put together a great list of kitchen utensil necessities:

- Instant-read thermometer
- Rubber or silicone bowl scrapers
- Whisk
- Wood spoons
- Ladle
- Spatula
- Offset spatula
- Stainless-steel grater (we have a flat one to save room)
- Stainless-steel tongs
- Vegetable peeler

- Slotted spoon
- Cooking spoon
- Long-handled fork
- Kitchen shears
- Kitchen timer (unless there is one on your oven)
- Vegetable slicer
- Garlic press
- Citrus reamer
- Basting brush

- Wire skimmer
- Potato masher (which we also use to make guacamole)
- Pizza slicer
- Measuring spoons
- Dry measuring cups
- Rolling pin
- Kitchen scale
- Ice-cream scoop
- One good set of knives

The must-have cookware Brette recommends:

- 1½-quart saucepan with lid
- 4-quart saucepan with lid
- Cast-iron skillet
- Sauté pan
- Dutch oven with lid

- Stockpot with lid (ours also has a steamer insert, which saves storage space)
- Shallow roasting pan with rack

We also have the following small appliances, which have allowed me to make any recipe I want. Of course, this could be adjusted for your family's lifestyle. For example, you might also want:

- a pasta maker or bread maker
- Large Crock-Pot with locking lid
- Small Crock-Pot for things such as cheese dip
- Waffle maker

- Mixer that doubles as a food processor
- A mini processor for small chopping jobs
- Toaster
- Toaster oven (we don't use a microwave)

Particularly if you live in a remote area, a well-stocked pantry is a necessity. Brette's list of foods to always have on hand will allow you to whip up *something* when you haven't planned ahead:

- Tomato paste
- Tomato sauce
- Canned whole tomatoes
- Canned diced tomatoes
- Tuna
- Canned soups
- Spaghetti sauce
- A variety of vegetables, either canned or frozen
- Chicken and beef broth (or vegetable if you're a vegetarian)
- Pickles
- Olives
- Salsa (jarred or your homemade canned or frozen)
- Pesto
- Canned, dried, or frozen fruit
- Applesauce
- An extra bag of dry and canned pet food. (This is so important, as we've run out or had a dog that wouldn't eat for some reason and we needed to whet their appetite with canned food). Having canned food is also good for emergencies when your pets must suddenly be on a wet diet.

I prefer many of my spices fresh now, but I do have Brette's recommended dried spices on hand too:

- Cayenne
- Chili powder
- Cinnamon (ground and stick)
- Cloves
- Cumin
- Curry powder
- Dill
- Garlic powder (I also have garlic salt)
- Ginger (ground)
- Nutmeg (ground)
- Onion powder
- Oregano
- Paprika
- Black peppercorns for your pepper grinder

- Red pepper flakes
- Rosemary
- Saffron

- Sage
- Tarragon
- Thyme
- Vanilla

We also have:

- Our favorite taco seasoning
- McCormick Grill Mates for meat on the grill

- McCormick Italian, Mexican, Mediterranean, and Asian seasonings

Visit my blog at LivingLargeinOurLittleHouse.com for some of our favorite recipes.

## LIVING LARGE TIPS: Saving Space in Your Little Kitchen

- Your kitchen doesn't need that "junk drawer" that is in so many kitchens. After eliminating the unnecessary clutter, we began using that drawer, which is the largest one, as our kitchen towel and wash cloth linen drawer.

- If you don't have a space-saving spice rack, put your spice jars in one of your drawers or use a magnetic rack that can go on your refrigerator or above your stove.

- Store your small appliances and leave you countertop space available for actual cooking. Doing this will also make your kitchen look less cluttered.

- Store your knives in a kitchen-counter block. (We received ours as a wedding gift.) This leaves room for other utensils in drawers.

- When designing your little home, try to incorporate both a lazy Susan and a cookie-sheet cabinet. These are awesome.

- Eliminate any doubles of your cooking gear.

- One item we've found to be one of our most treasured things in our little kitchen is the GelPro Elite mat that we put in front of our cabinets. As we've gotten older, Dale and I both have problems with plantar fasciitis, a painful foot condition. We both also have some lower back pain. When I do dishes by hand and stand chopping vegetables, my feet begin to hurt. Dale helps with dishes and cutting some vegetables, and he loves the mat too. I couldn't live without it now.

# 10

# Proximity Makes the Heart Grow Fonder:

## Growing and Staying Close-Knit with Your Family

*Living Truth: I've been asked about the key to a lasting relationship. It's not enough that Dale and I grew up together—it's also key that we've kept growing together.*

A grin on his face, Dale pointed the remote at me and acted like he was pushing the "off" button, like in the movie *Click*, in which a magical television remote puts people on pause. It was my turn to have the remote and decide what to watch, but he didn't want to give it up.

Television is our main form of entertainment in the winter, and because we only have one set, we take turns choosing shows.

When Dale and I lived in the split-level in the city, we had plenty of room to spread out. There were three bedrooms, a formal living room on the main floor, and a family room in the basement. We also had four televisions—one each in the kitchen, my office, our bedroom, and the family room.

Early in our marriage, we were too busy building our careers to watch much television. When we were home on weekends, we typically rented a movie. I did have to watch my taped episodes of the soap opera *All My Children* while we ate dinner on weeknights, which also made Dale a fan of the show. (Shh—don't tell!)

Later, when Dale began working nights, we never watched television together during the week. He came home about 3:30 a.m. and watched television to wind down, typically falling asleep on the floor in the basement family room because he said the floor felt good on his back. While he slept, I worked upstairs—conducting interviews on the phone and then preparing dinner—so the downstairs family room was cooler, darker, and quieter. We did watch some daytime television in the kitchen while we ate dinner before he left for work in the afternoon, but that was really just a habit of having *something* on while we ate.

Our living room can get quite cramped when all the dogs pile on!

After moving to Our Little House, we considered putting one of our televisions in the bedroom but decided against it. After all, we moved here to enjoy our lives and play outdoors, not to watch television.

I love my husband, and I'm sure he loves me. We grew up together, and we've built a good life for ourselves. We've been through some extraordinarily hard times together such as the losses of our loved ones, including my father, brother, and great-aunt, his grandmother, aunt, and uncle, and our mothers.

We've learned to revel in the good times and deal with the bad.

We don't argue about money or a silly thing like whether the toilet paper goes on to unfurl over or under—although we do have a running joke about which way it should go. He recently pointed out to me the story about the original patent intending it to go over, so I guess any dispute is now resolved for everyone, though I still just put it on, paying no attention to whether it's over or under.

But let me be clear. Sometimes being cooped up in Our Little House with my husband and five dogs is more challenging than anything we've dealt with in our almost 30-year marriage. This is true especially during the winter months. Although we had been married for 21 years by the time we moved to Our Little House, there were things I had either forgotten—because we had opposite schedules for so long—or just didn't know.

Dale loves action/adventure movies. The louder the better. I didn't realize, however, that he loves westerns as much as he seems to now. Dale works long hours, leaving by 5:15 in the morning six days a week and often not coming home until after 6 p.m.

As I've gotten older, I like blissful quiet. Sometimes I turn music or the radio on, but I usually work better when it is peaceful. Since the dogs typically don't say much—they only bark if they see the occasional squirrel or bird out the window or on the rare occasions that someone comes down the drive—that leaves me with just the voice in my head as I write. When I come home from a long day of writing, or especially when I get up in the morning, the last thing I want to hear is people screaming or loud, thunderous explosions.

Dale, of course, winds down differently. He spent many years working nights, coming home in the wee hours to decompress in front of the television downstairs. If the weather isn't agreeable to outdoor activities, he likes to spend the few hours he has at home watching television.

Since he worked nights, he probably didn't realize how much I *really* love true-crime drama. I spent a lot of evenings watching *Dateline*. I've also found a renewed passion for Kansas City Royals baseball. My family members were all huge fans of the game, and my mother first suspected she was pregnant with me at the home opener of the Kansas City A's season (long before the A's were in Oakland, they were the home team in Kansas City). My whole family spent many a weekend at Kauffman Stadium (now called The K) when I was a kid.

During the Royals' magical 2014 run to the World Series, my passion for the sport was renewed. However, Dale hates sports. All sports. This is fine with me when it comes to football, basketball, boxing, or car racing, but I'm still hoping to convert him to a baseball fan. He does relinquish the remote for important games such as post-season runs, and he'll go to an occasional game with me on our infrequent trips to Kansas City. I know that's true love; it's all about compromise.

I like my quiet Sunday mornings. Dale likes a good western. I like a Friday night spent with a true-crime drama or baseball game, while Dale prefers a thunderous, exploding action movie.

Somehow, we always work it out, and of course, this is only an issue during the winter months or in the terrible heat of deep summer when we can't be outside. Recording shows on the DVR is great. I can watch my shows while I eat lunch, and he can watch his after I go to bed on weekends. (I'm still an early bird, while he prefers to be a night owl on weekends.) If I don't feel like watching his choice of television, I have my iPod, my laptop, or a book. He has his magazines and projects, like restringing fishing line or tinkering with something that needs fixing. We can usually do separate things while still being together in one room.

Sure, life in Our Little House can be challenging at times, but overall, our relationship has become closer by being in close proximity to one another. However, having the Belle Writer's Studio for a retreat, should I need it—or one of the two outbuildings, should he—is a good idea for those times when we just need some time apart.

Hari Berzins—who lived in a tiny house with her husband, Karl, and two children—agrees that winters are the hardest season in a little home. Living in a tiny home, Hari says, "was like having a therapist. We had to work through things that came up. There were only so many places to retreat to, and negative energy can fill a space very fast, especially in the dead of winter. We learned to talk and even to yell—whatever it takes to work it out."

A potential conflict that trips up a lot of little house dwellers is when couples have different ideas about neatness. "My husband is messy and is kind of a hoarder, and I'm a clean freak," says Ramona DeAngelus. "It's magnified now because if he brings something into the tiny house, it messes up the whole space." The couple has found compromise by having a designated space on the windowsills for knickknacks, books and magazines.

## Sharing Space with Family

Someone recently asked me how our dogs get along in such tight quarters. Dale and I know that we have been extremely lucky with our dogs. Although they come from varied backgrounds and were rescued from different places at different times, they get along remarkably well. The few issues we've had have been solved with a few tricks I've learned over the years.

For example, when we first adopted Sade, the pittie, she was having issues with Emma, our only other large dog at the time. A quick call to some other pet writers led me to a trainer who works with rescued pit bulls. While I thought I was pampering Sade, the newcomer, by feeding her first, I was actually giving her dominance over me and Emma by letting her walk through the door first. This sent a message to her that she was the pack leader. When I started walking in the door first and feeding Emma before Sade, Sade seemed to recognize that I was in charge, and harmony was immediately restored.

The close quarters actually greatly improved the relationship between Dale and Molly, our little red dapple dachshund. Rescues can come with a variety of little quirks, and Molly was scared of men. Although Dale had never done anything to her, when she saw him walk into the living room at the split-level, she dove under the love seat to hide.

For four years, Dale would lie on the floor, lifting up the dust ruffle, trying to coax Molly out. Sometimes she would lick his fingers and finally relent. Sometimes she stayed hidden until he left the room. That all changed when we moved to Our Little House. With limited space to hide, Molly quickly gave up her phobia and enjoyed the rest of her days soaking in the love without the drama of having to be pulled out from underneath furniture.

Playing and having fun is an important part of life with the dogs. When we lived in the split-level, Dale would get on the floor and wrestle with Emma, which she loved. Sometimes Molly would forget herself and even join in the fun. We don't have room to wrestle on the floor with them now, but we do play games with them outside.

Jane Mosher, who raised her family in a small house in Canada, says that having fun was a key element in her family's ability to get along in their tight quarters. When her kids weren't out building snow forts and stick cabins in the woods, they found other ways to entertain themselves inside. "We had an old Ping-Pong table that was super heavy. It folded in half, and we stored it behind the freezer in the living room," Jane recalls. "When it came time to play, we hauled it out and propped it on the kitchen table. One player had the disadvantage of the freezer to their right; the other player had the disadvantage of the refrigerator to their right. But we played for hours and hours. Good memories."

Having children in a tiny home can be a challenge, but Bec Gawtry, who has twins, says she thinks it has helped her girls grow closer. "Sharing a bedroom has strengthened their bond; they have very few squabbles," Bec says. "When they were younger, we had them both in the same full-size bed, and they were always awake playing together. We now have bunk beds for them, which gives them each their own space, but also creates a boundary when needed."

Archer and Ella Berzins practice instruments while their father, Karl, cooks dinner in their tiny home.

Hari Berzins agrees that the opportunity for her children to share a room allowed her kids to grow close. "Our kids play together all the time and engage in pretend play, which has also helped them develop their imaginations," she says.

Everyone I interviewed for this book said the exact same things about maintaining a healthy relationship with family inside a tiny home: Communication is essential and compromise is imperative.

While Dale and I have grown closer to each other and with our dogs, it has been more difficult staying close with loved ones and family who don't live nearby. When we moved from our home in Kansas City, we moved more than 300 miles away from the people we'd known all our lives. The only people we knew well here were my Aunt Kathy and her husband Monty.

After we built Our Little House, we initially came down every other weekend. Those trips were so short, and we didn't have any extra space for visitors to sleep, so we never had guests on those trips. However, after we moved here full-time, we envisioned being busy with visiting family and friends, sitting around the fire pit or on the deck.

Really, who wouldn't want to be in paradise *with us*?

Dale and I have been outdoor people for so long that we never stopped to think when we moved that most of our loved ones weren't outdoor people. Their idea of fun isn't jumping at the chance to drive six hours to be in the middle of the woods with ticks and snakes. The bonus of seeing us didn't seem to be a better draw. Even our friends who *do* enjoy the outdoors are busy and have limited time for vacations. While they've spent some time with us, they don't want to spend every vacation here.

♦

In the first year we lived at Our Little House, we made it back to Kansas City three or four times for visits. A lot of my work was still tied to our hometown, so I also traveled there several times on business. As my business transitioned further away from Kansas City publications, it seems our visits did as well. Work and life and the activities we moved *here* for keep us from too many visits "home."

It seems the simple answer would be to expand our circle of friends here. Easier said than done, however, especially for people beyond their 20s. According to a study published in 2013 in the Psychological Bulletin, the older we get, the fewer friends we have.[25] It's also hard to make friends in middle age because we're too busy either working or taking care of our elderly parents—or both—to devote the time it takes to create and nurture lasting friendships. As well, those same studies suggest we may be more set in our ways than we realize, making it harder to accept people who don't fit our established values.

Combine our age with our very rural location—and the fact that we're both basically introverts—let's just say making friends has been difficult.

This is something to consider when leaving your family and friends for the rural life. We do have a couple sets of friends here now, and I keep trying to make more by getting out of the Belle Writer's Studio more often. I've taken classes in plant-based cooking, pottery, and Tai Chi. But these classes were in a town 50 minutes away, and most of the people who take them are too. But taking classes, even if they don't net any lasting relationships, is mostly about learning new things and enjoying new adventures, which is part of Living Large.

## EXPERT TIPS: Irene Levine

Irene Levine, a relationship expert and founder of TheFriendshipBlog.com, offers these tips for making new friends if you're moving to a new community to live in your little home:

- **Reach out to your nearby neighbors.** They'll be curious about the "new people" next door, so it's a great time to introduce yourself. Exchange phone numbers and let them know they can count on you in an emergency, and hopefully, you'll be able to do the same.

- **Follow your interests.** Try to get engaged in community, religious, or civic activities that appeal to you. Those are the places where you are likely to find kindred spirits. Join a gym or book club, volunteer, or take an adult-education class.

- **Find out whether there is a "newcomers' club."** Many communities have them.

- **Check out whether there are any Meetup.com groups in your community.** If not, start one focused on your interests (e.g., cooking, photography, etc.).

- **Give yourself time.** Go slowly. Don't expect too much too soon. Make acquaintances first that may turn into friends. Anything you can do regularly, where you see the same people week after week, makes it easier to develop a friendship.

- **Don't be afraid to make the first move.** What could possibly happen except that the other person may already have all the friends he or she needs? Don't take rejection personally.

- **Use the warm weather seasons** to get out of your house and put yourself in the position to meet new people.

- **Don't give up on your old friends.** Stay in touch online or by phone, and keep up with the most significant events in their lives. Invite them to see your new home and visit them periodically.

---

**LIVING LARGE TIPS:** Staying Close and Connected

---

- Have realistic expectations of your new home. The culture might be very different from what you were used to in the city, even if the rural area is less than 100 miles from the city. Embrace the nuances and don't fight it.

- Find local people with similar interests on social media, which can eventually lead to real-life friendships.

- Make plans to go home and reconnect with family and friends often, especially when you first move, and make sure they also have open invitations for visits.

# 11

# A Real Treat
# When You Know the Tricks:
## Entertaining and Decorating
## for Holidays

*Living Truth: Our stockings are hung from the door handles with care . . .
because if we hung them from the woodstove, they would probably catch fire.*

When I was about 9, my nephew Keith was at our house for an overnight stay. We made a game of lying underneath the huge artificial Christmas tree in our living room at the bungalow, counting the lights from that vantage point.

The lights kept him mesmerized for what seemed like a long time, especially for a four-year-old. That night, he eventually fell asleep under the tree. I still remember how sweet he looked sleeping there with the glow of the tree lights hitting his face, but I mostly remember how small he looked under that *huge* tree.

When I was growing up, Christmas was an event. My dad would secure the huge six-foot artificial tree to the wall in the bungalow so it wouldn't tip over. The decorations took up about a third of the formal living room, and when presents were wrapped and under the tree, free space was practically nonexistent. My mom and dad loved Christmas, and as typical Depression-era parents, they wanted their family to have more than an orange and a small toy to open.

After we moved to the Wilson House, the Christmas decorations grew along with the size of the real estate. The big tree was put out on the four-season porch, and two other smaller trees decorated the living room and my bedroom. My mother's gift-wrapping was an art. She wrapped the presents in the prettiest papers she could find, bound them with ribbon and bows, and sometimes even added little decorations. The gifts were so beautiful that we *almost* didn't want to open them.

When my mother passed away, she still had most of her Christmas decorations, including a very large nativity scene and boxes full of post–World War II decorations. I also had my own decorations from many years of marriage. I liked decorating for not only Christmas, but for all of the holidays. I had plenty of Halloween and Easter decor, St. Patrick's, Valentine's Day—there wasn't a popular holiday for which I didn't decorate.

When we decided to live permanently in Our Little House, I realized I would never decorate for the holidays as I once had. We were so cramped that first winter—with our 10-by-10-foot bedroom doubling as my office and a filing cabinet in the living room— that I didn't decorate at all.

Our bears get dressed up for Christmas.

I have since learned that this is not uncommon for people in their first year of tiny house living. "The first year we had our kids in our small house, we didn't decorate for Christmas at all," says Bec Gawtry. "We felt like it would be a disaster, and we didn't get an artificial tree because there isn't room to store it."

The family now decorates a small live tree, but the bigger celebration happens outdoors. "We use our outdoor space for decorating," says Bec. "We have lights everywhere, even along the fence. It is a big deal for the girls, and they get so excited when we turn on the lights."

Some new small house dwellers do decorate their first year in their new home, sometimes with mixed results. Twentysomethings Alyson (Ally) and Aaron Courain didn't have much accumulated Christmas decor when they moved into their 620-square-foot lakefront cottage near Wharton, New Jersey. Aaron says that people who don't know the area get a false idea of their part of the country. "When people think of New Jersey, they tend to think of densely populated areas," says Aaron. "It's not like that at all in northwest New Jersey. We have access to the lake and 100 acres of woods."

The giant picture window in the living room of Alyson and Aaron Courain's 620-square-foot cottage offers sweeping views of Lake Shawnee, in northwest New Jersey.

Since the couple loves being outdoors and going on weekend adventures, a little house fits their lifestyle. Aaron, an engineer, also finds that the compact cottage suits his efficient personality.

Their cottage has a great picture window with a view of their 300-square-foot deck and the lake beyond. The first Christmas they lived in their little lake home, Aaron was in charge of getting the tree, which they planned to put on the deck. "Ally made some homemade popcorn strings," Aaron says. "The problem was that the squirrels kept eating the popcorn, and the wind kept blowing over the tree. We were going out two times a day just to prop the tree back up."

Alyson grew up having a big tree in her family home, and that's what she expected to have when she married. "After that first year, we decided to do a mini tree in the house," she says. The couple also decorates inside the home. For example, a pin board in the kitchen is transformed into a holiday decoration, and they hang stockings on the mantel and string garland throughout the house.

Alyson and Aaron Courain's festive holiday decorations include a mini Christmas tree displayed in their living room picture window.

Like the Gawtrys and Courains, Dale and I were ready for the holidays when the second year rolled around. Paring down my collection of decorations came easily when I realized that some items that had been stored were ruined by mildew.

As I shared before, Our Little House is decorated in a bear theme, and we like sticking to a single concept, as it works better in such a small space. We purchased a small artificial pine tree that looks as if it's been cut from the woods outside our door and new small tree ornaments with a bear or outdoor theme. I kept one antique ornament that was on my mom's tree, and bought a few miniature post–World War II ornaments from antique stores just to add a touch of tradition to the tree.

We hang our stockings on the two pulls on our laundry room doors. (We can't hang them on a mantel when we have a woodstove.) I also decorate our kitchen table and use holiday-themed night-lights in the kitchen and bathroom.

Most of our big decorating happens outside. Although I could never get Dale to hang Christmas lights when we lived in the city, I converted him to recognizing the beauty of the lights when they glow in our woods. We hang them on our Party Deck and on the covered front porch at the Belle Writer's Studio. When surrounded by darkness, they are breathtakingly lovely. Dale enjoys seeing them when he arrives home from work or when we come home from an evening of errands.

🏠

Before we put up the Christmas decor, though, there is decorating for autumn. For that season, nature offers the best resources. Sue Smith Moak has a great idea for autumn decorating. She uses real pumpkins and winter squash. "I can use them for food afterward and don't have to worry about storing them for later," she says.

I also used nature's bounty, typically getting some colorful mums for the deck. I go a little more commercial, hanging purchased Halloween wreaths on our doors and displaying ceramic jack-o'-lanterns inside Our Little House and the studio.

For other holidays, I like to decorate our front and back doors. I've also amassed a small collection of wind socks, another fun outdoor holiday decoration. And, of course, the "Happy Everything" sign my mom made for me many years ago hangs near our back door year-round, reminding us to celebrate every holiday and every day.

Sue Smith Moak's homemade autumnal decorations cheerfully greet visitors arriving at her rural Texas cabin.

## Having a Tiny Home Doesn't Mean You Can't Entertain

When Dale and I were first married, my family always ate Christmas dinner and opened presents on December 24, a tradition from the German side of my mom's family. Early in their marriage, my parents had tried the "American" way—opening gifts on Christmas morning—until they got tired of getting woken up in the middle of the night by excited kids. After that, they moved subsequent celebrations to Christmas Eve, telling us that we were first on Santa's list so he delivered gifts to us early.

When we lived in the bungalow, Mom hosted either Thanksgiving or Christmas, and my oldest sister hosted the other holiday. You would think hosting at least 13 people would be crazy in an 800-square-foot house. But Mom just moved furniture, added the leaves to dining-room table, and the adults, at least, all fit around the table. The kids ate at a separate table in the kitchen. Large holiday celebrations can be enjoyed in a little home—it just takes a little planning.

Dale and I no longer have those large celebrations. Most of our older relatives are gone, and we live so far from other family that it's typically just the two of us. I often miss the holiday sprints we used to do, hitting all of our family's homes. It wasn't about the presents or the food, but we miss those people who have passed. Still, Living Large is about living in the moment with who and what we have.

If Dale and I don't get back home to Kansas City for the holidays, we typically just make a special dinner for the two of us. This usually is homemade tacos on Thanksgiving. We don't buy each other Christmas presents, as we don't need anything, but we celebrate Christmases past and present with a very miniature version of the traditional meal we enjoy: mashed sweet potatoes with marshmallows, ham, hash-brown casserole, green beans, and rolls. Dale generally has several days off, and we use the time to get things done around Our Little House. If we're lucky, the unpredictable Ozarks weather will hold out, and we can still take the boat on the lake or go for a hike.

The spectacular view from the deck of Alyson and Aaron Courain's little home provides a stunning backdrop for outdoor entertaining in summer or winter.

Having a tiny home doesn't mean you can't entertain family and friends—at the holidays or anytime. The Courains love entertaining in their 620-square-foot house in New Jersey, especially in winter—and just not on the holidays. They have hosted as many as twenty-five guests in the winter. Their secret to accommodating a big crowd?

They are not afraid to utilize the outdoors, even when it's cold. Aaron and Alyson get an outside fire roaring and set up benches on their expansive deck, complete with heated blankets. "We also provide baskets with more blankets and throws if people need them," says Alyson.

However, activities are not limited to sitting around the fire trying to stay warm. "We still use the full extent of the lake, even in the winter," says Aaron. "We go ice-skating, cross-country skiing, and it's really great because it gets people out doing activities they may not normally do."

Bec Gawtry and her family in Minnesota haven't tried hosting Doug's very large family for holidays in their little house, but she has hosted her parents, brother, and his family. "If we're hosting, we go sledding in the park so we aren't all cooped up in the house the entire time," she says.

The right furniture can be the key to entertaining. We have a small drop-leaf table that seats two when the leaves are down, and four to six people when the leaves are up. Many tiny home dwellers have custom-designed tables that fold down when not in use, but can be folded out when entertaining during the holidays or anytime.

Folding tables, like the one seen here in Tammy Strobel's tiny house, can be a boon to entertaining, or just living.

Entertaining in a small space is all about not setting expectations too high, preparing, planning, and having the right furniture. The gatherings might be smaller and more intimate, but like everything else in a small house, this could be an advantage.

---

**LIVING LARGE TIPS:** Entertaining in a Small Space

---

- Even if you're eating and doing the bulk of entertaining outside, Alyson Courain advises that you keep the food inside and spread it out buffet-style on the counters.

- Try doing all the food preparation yourself. While it may seem like more work, it could save you anxiety in the kitchen later. "If guests come with food, it gets more cluttered and stressful," Alyson says. "Also, if they need to warm food and you have limited space, it gets even more stressful."

- Know your limits. If Aaron and Alyson have to entertain inside due to really inclement weather, they feel their comfort limit is between six and 10 people.

- Be organized and try to have everything ready in advance of your guests' arrival.

# 12

# Grandma's Cabinet
## Takes Up Half the Room:
# Finding Homes for Heirlooms

*Living Truth*: *Less stuff = more life.*

When I was a kid, Sunday mornings, like all mornings, began with my parents reading the newspaper. But instead of politics and world news, on Sundays they were mostly interested in the classifieds section of the paper, seeking out antique auctions.

When my parents remodeled the bungalow in 1974, Mom decorated the kitchen and family room in country antiques. On her Sunday adventures, she had found a very large, old spinning wheel that adorned the living room, a wood spice cabinet, a dry sink, a large pie safe, and a butter churn.

She also bought and decorated travel trunks for each of her daughters, where we would keep our mementos; various benches and chairs; as well as a full ice-cream parlor set with the marble tabletop that is now on our covered front porch.

To say my mom was a little obsessed with antiques would be an understatement. All these pieces of furniture worked well in the Wilson House, with its early-twentieth-century architecture. My mom kept most of them as she moved through the years. She did give me the spinning wheel as a housewarming gift when we purchased the split-level.

Mom willed anything that was gifted to her back to the giver, but willed to me most everything that she purchased on those Sunday antiquing trips that the three of us made together. When we moved to Our Little House and decided to make it our permanent residence, I knew I wouldn't have room for most of my mom's beloved antiques.

After having been moved numerous times, most of the antiques had been damaged or—like the spinning wheel—broken, so they weren't worth having appraised or selling. Some of the pieces had such strong memories attached that I could not bear to part with them, like the electrified silver oil lamp on my bedside table. I can't remember it ever not being on Mom's bedside table.

The lamp was there when I was little. When I'd get up from nightmares and go into my parents' room, my mom would turn it on and comfort me.

As a teen, I would pop my head into the doorway of their bedroom, first at the little bungalow and then at the Wilson House. My mom would be reading; the light would be on; and cigarette smoke would be swirling around it. "Good night, Mamma. I'll see you in the morning." Mom would look up at me over her reading glasses, "Good night, sweetie. Sleep tight. Don't let the bedbugs bite!"

Memories like that are priceless and make an ordinary piece an heirloom. And an heirloom like this lamp makes a house a home. But we knew we didn't have room for it all.

A friend of mine, Candy Barnes, once wrote on social media after she finished remodeling and decorating her new home, "If we surround ourselves with the things we love, the things that make us happy, the things that give us pleasure, then we will always have an oasis to retreat to in times of stress."

My mother's lamp and antique dresser help make our bedroom more homey.

Since we initially didn't plan on Our Little House being our full-time residence, I didn't have the opportunity to design special places for some of the antiques I loved. I had to decide which of my mother's heirlooms I couldn't live without and then figure out a way to incorporate them into our new space. Some of the smaller things were relatively easy to find space for, such as two of my grandmother's serving bowls and my mom's crystal decanter that she used for vinegar.

Other things were more difficult to find homes for, such as the antique washstand, which now holds my coffee maker in the Belle Writer's Studio, as well as my mother's antique dresser, which is really too big for our bedroom. One can tell that it isn't an expensive piece—it was probably even handcrafted by someone for his own home—but it provides space for some of our necessary clothing and has two little drawers on the top (at either side) for some of my jewelry and small keepsakes.

My mother's antique washstand found a home in the Belle Writer's Studio.

I kept my dad's footlocker from World War II with the "F. Fivecoat" stencil still visible, the trunk my mom made for my keepsakes, and my mom's travel trunk, in which she kept old family albums and photographs.

I still don't know what to do with most of it, including my mother's wedding china, her red Christmas dinnerware, and that old pie safe. No one in the family has antique decor or a home that would accommodate such large pieces of furniture. Also, postings on sites dedicated to tiny house living and even articles in mainstream media suggest that many Millennials just aren't interested in collecting a bunch of stuff.[26] This is perhaps why so many young people are interested in tiny house living; many don't have an attachment to stuff that previous generations have.

That isn't true, however, for young people who have memories attached to specific family heirlooms. Aaron and Alyson Courain describe themselves basically as minimalists, but they do have two sets of her grandmother's dishes stored in their basement. "It takes up a lot of real estate, but I just can't get rid of it," says Alyson.

People of all generations often still want to keep family photos. Sue Smith Moak wanted to keep as many of her memories as close as possible. She copied all of her family photographs and gave most of the originals to her adult children, who are Millennials. "I scanned all of the photos and just kept a few in binders and albums," Sue says. "I had photo books made with special photos and they take up just a little room."

Dale and I still have a lot of pieces that belonged to my mother. When we moved, it had been only a few months since she had passed away. I wasn't yet ready to give up even the pieces I knew I would never use, even if I had the room, such as her dining room set, where we had celebrated many holiday meals, the headboard to her bed, and that painting of the French countryside Mom had purchased to put over the mantel at the Wilson House.

We spent thousands of dollars and a lot of time storing those items, moving them, and then storing them again. Time has allowed me to finally reconcile the fact that my parents aren't what they owned. I can have the memories of them in my heart and photos of the things that helped make our lives together special in my mind—without having the physical clutter.

We are working right now to get rid of most of it from the storage building on our property, but it was an expensive lesson for us.

Like many tiny house dwellers, letting go of heirlooms was the hardest part for Hari Berzins and her family. "We got rid of that stuff last," says Hari. "We took photos of each item we were letting go and wrote the story of each item and put it with the photo. We still own the memories. It's not the thing that's important—it's those memories that went with it."

Another option is to give heirlooms away as gifts, if you know people who would appreciate them. We gave a blond wood cedar chest that belonged to my mother to my godmother's grandson as a wedding gift. Their home is decorated in a retro-midcentury style with blond wood, so it was the perfect new home for our chest.

When we delivered the piece to Quinn and Michael after their wedding, they were thrilled. I told Quinn that it had an indirect tie to his beloved granny, as his Grandma Grace and my mother had been best friends. I could imagine my mom showing off her new cedar chest. "Who knows?" I told Quinn. "Your granny may have even helped pick it out." The cedar chest is living a new life as a table in their living room.

---

**LIVING LARGE TIPS:** Getting Rid of Heirlooms

---

- If you have younger relatives who share an interest in antiques or passing family heirlooms to their own children, allow them to have first dibs. But professional organizer Janine Adam says, "Give them a deadline to get it. Don't let them make you keep it and store it forever."

- Consider donating items to a worthy cause, such as a favorite charity or your local historical society. "Just because it's an heirloom, it doesn't mean you can't donate it," says Janine.

- Finally, if you don't want to donate it, sell it online or through an auction. You might just get enough from your items to pay for your tiny home!

# 13

# You Only Have One Life:
## Following Your Passions

*Living Truth*: *"I've never found time spent amongst nature
to be a waste of time."*

**—UNKNOWN**

When Dale and I began dating, we would often visit Wyandotte County Lake Park, a 1,500-acre park with a 400-acre lake located on the western edge of Kansas City, Kansas. Sometimes we'd meet up with friends and grill hamburgers and steaks, or sometimes we'd go on romantic picnics and hikes by ourselves. In the winter, we'd drive through the park hoping to spot an eagle, since they frequented the park that time of the year. We even had our wedding reception in the reception hall on the park grounds.

We were, from the beginning, outdoor people. After we got married, we got into fishing. I hadn't fished a lot, but my dad had quite the collection of antique wooden lures he had fished with when he was a kid. However, he had long given up the hobby by the time I came along. Dale had grown up fishing and hunting with his grandfather and dad. Dale and I began bank fishing, and I was immediately hooked, so to speak.

We got off work in the evenings and took our dachshund, Hershey, with us to the nearest little pond at Pierson Park, which was closer than Wyandotte County Lake and perfect for a couple of hours of fishing after work. We would fish until dark. It was on one of those outings that we discovered Hershey couldn't swim. As Dale cast out his line with the bobber, Hershey watched intently and, before we knew it, jumped into the water and was wading out to retrieve the bobber. Suddenly, she stopped, looked back at us, and flipped over on her back and went under. I couldn't get a word out before Dale was in the water, going after her.

She was only out about eight feet, a little above waist-high for Dale, and he scooped her up and brought her back to shore. She was fine, but the brand-new athletic shoes Dale had on were ruined.

Before our next outing, we went to the pet-supply store and found a cute little pink life jacket for her. She never went near the water without it again. Soon after, we bought our first boat, the 1979 *Sea Nymph* and began taking it out to Wyandotte County Lake every Sunday. Hershey became known as the "dog with the pink life jacket" by the park rangers at Wyandotte County Lake.

The *Sea Nymph*; Hershey in her pink life jacket.

In our little blue-collar community, "lake life" was something to aspire to. Many people had bought lake lots, mostly at Lake of the Ozarks in Missouri, in hopes of building their retirement homes. My godparents had a mobile home on a lot at a private lake for those who had worked at the railroad. My parents bought a lot at a smaller lake in Kansas, but of course, their retirement dreams were derailed.

When Dale and I first visited my aunt Kathy and Monty here on their property, we had only fished Bull Shoals Lake a few times. We had fished nearby Table Rock many times, while staying at cabins there during vacations, and we loved the vastness of the water. We loved Bull Shoals even more, because its water is crystal clear and many of its areas have yet to be developed.

An aerial view of Bull Shoals Lake.

I had always wanted to have a permanent lake home. When my aunt presented us with the opportunity, we jumped at the chance. Hershey made our fishing adventures even more fun, and when we first built Our Little House and came down for weekends, she was just as happy as we were to be by the water. Seeing her in her cute little pink life jacket deepened our love for being at the lake.

Dale and I are both squeamish about killing and eating fish. As Dale once said after killing the fish he caught and cooking them right away, "That's just a little too fresh." We typically just catch and release. Being on the water is the thrill for me and I'm fine with just sitting and watching the wildlife on shore, or lying back in the boat and watching the clouds roll by.

On sunny Sunday mornings between May and October, you can usually find us on the water. On Sunday afternoons, after a long morning of fishing and boating, we are usually hanging out on our Party Deck. Dale loves to grill and do outdoor cast-iron cooking. He cooks enchilada casserole and cobblers in his Dutch ovens, and there is nothing better than his cooking. The food is definitely part of "Sunday Funday" at Our Little House.

We have tried to fully embrace the lake life we had envisioned for ourselves. Sometimes it's truly like being on a camping trip that never ends. We walk the dogs on our country road and hike a few of the trails in the state parks and national forests that border Our Little House. We take the four-wheeler down to the lake point at the end of our road, walk the shoreline, and marvel at the beauty of the water. We hope to take a couple of fishing poles with us on those rides this summer and do a little bank fishing in the evenings, as we used to so long ago with Hershey.

We love that living in the country allows us to go boating, fishing, or hiking anytime we want.

Our rural yard also makes for some interesting days watching wildlife. At night, we listen to it while sitting on the deck. We have a wildlife cam, which we set up deep in our woods every winter to see what we can "shoot." We don't hunt, so this is the only way animals on our land might get "shot." Mostly we see deer, as we lure them with corn. Last winter, we did capture a squirrel that kept frequenting the corn we scattered. In one shot, he is sitting atop the camera peering down into the lens as if taking a selfie. Once, we caught a very large coyote on camera. It was so large that a friend thought it might be some sort of a wolf hybrid (although wolves are not thought to be in Arkansas). I took the photo to the local conservation department, and they determined that it was, in fact, "a very large and very healthy coyote."

We also have a little wren that nests on our covered front porch every spring. She's been here for the past four years or so. Last spring, her babies had already hatched when we heard her raising quite a commotion. Dale went outside but couldn't find the source of her angst. She kept it up, squawking loudly.

Dale looked around again and found a small black snake on the table near where she was nesting. He grabbed the long tongs he uses for handling charcoal while cooking outdoors, picked up the snake, carried it up the road, and relocated it on the opposite side. The next day, I went outside and saw a huge black snake, about six feet long, heading toward the porch. These snakes really wanted to snack on those baby birds. Fortunately, black snakes are not poisonous, nor are they typically very aggressive.

I'm not as brave as Dale when it comes to snakes that large, as they still bite, so I grabbed the broom and shooed it away from the house. As we've learned, all the creatures here have a place in the chain. Black snakes are "good" snakes, in that they eat the mice and wood rats. They will eat poisonous snakes as well. We hated to shoo these black snakes away, but we felt the need to protect our returning wren and her little brood. We love most of the wildlife here and don't kill anything unless it is threatening to us or our dogs.

Of course, finding your passions is also about discovering what you're not passionate about. The first (and only) time we rented a canoe on the Buffalo River, about an hour from our house, it wasn't long before Dale was complaining that I wasn't doing my share of the paddling and that he was doing all the work. When the boat started to lean,

I instinctively leaned with it and promptly tipped us over, sending us into the warm August water.

"What did you do that for?" Dale said as he surfaced.

"Well, it wasn't like I meant to," I replied, trying to scramble for our waterproof camera. Everything was supposed to be secured in the boat, but the camera wasn't and it was now floating downstream. We quickly learned why the locals call canoeing "the divorce boat."

While on a travel-writing assignment, I tried kayaking a tributary leading into the Gulf of Mexico, and although the boat was somewhat hard to get in and out of for a middle-aged woman with back and knee issues, I really liked it. Yearning for a new adventure, Dale and I took a formal kayaking class on Bull Shoals Lake and found we loved it. We hope to add kayaking to our list of regular activities on the lake.

When I am homesick for Kansas City, feel down, or experience cabin fever in the winter, I close my eyes and think of sitting in the boat on the lake on a misty morning. The lake is truly our church. Nowhere else on earth can bring us the peace we feel while floating on the water. The only sounds are the occasional birdcall or a wild animal rustling in the weeds onshore. I open my eyes and envision that sign on the wall across from the futon and remember that, indeed, "Life Is Good."

It's not surprising that all of the tiny house dwellers I've encountered are outdoor people. We would rather be doing something outdoors than sitting inside. That's certainly the case for Ramona and Carlo DeAngelus. Call Ramona's telephone, and if she doesn't pick up, you'll hear her chipper voice-mail message: "If we're not here, we're outside doing something awesome!"

When I called them and heard that message, it was a spring evening and they were out hunting ramps (wild leeks). "Our philosophy is that we're here and we want to have a good time and a good life," Ramona says. She likes to garden and says Carlo is always outside working on a DIY project.

Ramona and Carlos enjoying their outdoor patio.

Sue Smith Moak writes a blog called A Porch of My Own (www.rockinrsranch.blogspot.com) about life on her property, but she and her husband, Rick, didn't envision spending most of their retirement sitting on their comfortable porch in their rocking chairs. They envisioned hunting their property, gardening, fishing, and staying active. Rick was an avid outdoorsman and hunter. Sue is handy around the house and built their outdoor furniture from wood left over from other projects and upcycled items. The result is a comfortable outdoor entertainment area. When she isn't watching wildlife or enjoying the antics of her longhorns, Gus and Woodrow, she is still keeping active with small building projects.

Sue Smith Moak built the furniture in her outdoor living space using wood scraps and upcycled objects.

The fun really begins when her family comes for visits. "I spend a lot of my free time outdoors having fun, which is something Rick and I weren't able to do before, because we were spending so much time working on the house and the yard," she says. "Now, I can go to the river at the state park near the ranch and canoe and tube with the grandkids and friends."

Aaron and Alyson Courain don't let the seasons affect their outdoor life. They enjoy winter sports around their lake property just as much as summer adventures. They bike, hike, fish, mountain climb, and take road trips almost every weekend in the summer, and ice-skate, hike, and find other adventures in the winter. "Our house is very comfortable, but it has made us spend more time outside," says Aaron. "When your home is cozy, it helps motivate you to get outside and not become couch potatoes, and because the rent is cheap, we have more money to do what we love."

Aaron and Alyson Courain enjoy lake activities all year round.

🏠

Misti McCloud's passion is riding motorcycles. She chose the area where she rented a vacation cabin for a winter, near the Pisgah National Forest in the mountains of western North Carolina, because of the scenic routes around the home. "The roads are amazing for riding," she says. "I don't have to work as hard to pay for rent and utilities, so I can spend my life actually living."

Misti McCloud loves riding near her little winter home.

🏠

Perhaps no one incorporates their passions into their lives as much as people who live on a houseboat and sail the world, as Diane Selkirk and her family have done. "Because our home moves, we can see a lot of the world while living affordably," says Diane. The family has sailed near Central America, crossed the South Pacific, and visited Indonesia, Malaysia, and Thailand.

People believe the sailing lifestyle has a lot of risks, but for Diane's family, there has been only one instance when they were truly frightened. On one trip, they were hit by a violent storm just after arriving in Puerto Vallarta. They managed to drop anchor in a crowded port, but this can be dangerous when the sea is blowing boats around. "For about 45 minutes, we had hurricane-force winds," says Diane. "Boats were colliding with each other and being blown up on the beach."

Diane put their then eight-year-old daughter Maia into a life jacket, then put Charlie the cat in a backpack and had them sit near the door in case they needed to abandon their sailboat. Luckily, the family and the boat weathered the storm without any major damage. Aside from losing a rudder while crossing the South Pacific once, they haven't had any other scary instances in all their time sailing, which most likely speaks to their many years of sailing experience

Diane says they wouldn't give up the experiences of seeing the world for anything. "Maia's done more in her years of sailing than many people do in a lifetime," says Diane. And that is what Living Large is all about.

Diane Selkirk and her family have pursued their passion for traveling by exploring the world—including French Polynesia—in their tiny home, a 40-foot catamaran.

## LIVING LARGE TIPS: Following Your Passions in a Small House

- If you're an outdoor person, take some primitive-camping trips. What does this have to do with living your passions from a tiny house? Taking only what you truly need on primitive-camping trips helps you see how much you really need—and how much you can do without—when paring down for your tiny home life.

- One of my passions is our dogs. If your passion is rescuing animals or even having farm animals, do your research and know your limitations. After we had lived here for three years, I began volunteering with a rescue group, and I realized that I *really* can't turn away when an animal is in imminent danger. We learned that six or seven dogs stretches our budget pretty thin. The simple act of having a goat or getting chickens isn't as easy as it looks. Avoid having more animals than you can physically or financially care for.

- If you are moving to a lake for the "lake life" and a boat is a part of your plan, make sure it is also a part of your Living Large budget. Remember, it's fine to have stuff if that stuff actually brings you joy. If I had to choose, I would give up my car before I would give up my dogs or our boat.

- If you have a hobby that requires equipment, such as mountain biking or kayaking, plan for storage space. The Courains, for example, store all their equipment in their basement. Some tiny house dwellers store their equipment in an unused loft or hang bikes and other equipment from the ceiling. Others who have the room store their equipment in dedicated sheds or garages.

## 14

# Petite Can Be Professional:
# Working from Your Little House

*Living Truth: I owe, I owe, so off to work I go!*
*At least it's only up the driveway.*

When I was sitting in my gray corporate cube back in the 1990s, I would dream of having a tiny writer's cabin tucked back in the woods. I could envision myself inside the little log cabin, typing away on a story or a manuscript. Every once in a while, I would look up and gaze at the beauty of the lake and woods, smiling as Dale made another cast from our dock while Hershey ran around in her little pink life jacket, barking at the bobber. Our Blazer would be parked nearby, and there would be a canoe sitting up on the shore.

I knew from the moment I got my first corporate job that I wasn't cut out for sitting in a gray cubicle for eight to 10 hours a day, analyzing other people's credit reports and making collection calls. I sure wasn't cut out to manage people or play office politics. After my dad died, I had given up the dream of attending the University of Kansas and going to journalism school. There wasn't enough money for tuition, and the one-hour commute from the Wilson House would have required me to live on campus, which was additional money we didn't have.

It took me 10 years of working full-time and going to school part-time, but I finally earned my bachelor's degree in the winter of 1992, making me the first in my family to have a four-year degree.

During that period, I also transferred from J.C. Penney, where I worked in the credit department, to the credit-processing center, which began my dozen-year journey in credit call centers.

While I daydreamed in that cubicle about my dream job in the cabin, I was also making plans to make that dream come true. I attended local writing workshops, and after I finished my degree, took writing classes. One early fall day, the higher-ups at the bank call center gathered us together to inform us that our department was being eliminated. We were "JD'd," as they called it in corporate speak, meaning "Job Discontinued."

I had been so unhappy during that time that I had begun taking antidepressants and wearing a night guard while I slept so I wouldn't break my teeth from grinding them so hard. When we heard the news of our department's demise, it was hard at first to give up the security of a full-time job, which is what I'd known all of my professional life. I initially made a couple of half-hearted attempts at applying for jobs in other departments before I accepted that it was time for me to move on.

I empathized with my coworkers, who were fretting over the loss of our jobs. But I was silently counting the days until I would be free of the corporate cube and could start my professional life as a freelance writer. During those thirty days of waiting until my last day, I actually did a little happy dance when I got into my car at the end of each day.

I was able to begin that journey to my writing cabin in the woods on one of my favorite holidays—Halloween—in 1998, a day I'll forever recognize as my "Free Day," the day I was emancipated from a corporate life I hated to pursue a profession I love. To me, being a writer is truly an adventure. In my research for stories, I've had the opportunity to put on a lab coat, booties, and hairnet to watch fertility specialists begin the process of creating human life in a petri dish. Dale and I spent the night in Jesse James's boyhood home in hopes of catching his ghost; we stayed in a reportedly haunted hotel, and I found my heart racing when we captured unexplained balls of light with our camera. (These are thought by people who believe in ghosts to be orbs or spirits.)

I've had the chance to write about animals, one of my deepest passions. I wrote about the pit-bull rescue that took more than a dozen of Michael Vick's dogs from the horror of that dog-fighting operation and gave them a new life full of love. I followed the new lives of some of those dogs as they transitioned from the terrible abuse they suffered as fighting dogs to their new lives as beloved family members. I've also written about their deaths in old age, as they passed into the next world not surrounded by abuse and violence, but by the love of their adoptive families.

Almost every day, I talk to interesting people on the phone, such as the investigator who caught the BTK (Bind, Torture, Kill) serial killer in Wichita, Kansas, and the soldier who fought to bring home Ratchet, the dog she rescued while serving in Iraq.

Being self-employed has given me the freedom to have adventures outside of my home office. On assignment for stories on family history, I've traveled from the wonders of the Great Smoky Mountains, where I was able to visualize where my paternal ancestors may have originated, to the city streets of South Side Chicago, where my maternal family lived until the Great Depression drove them to my great-grandfather's farm.

I've seen where my maternal grandfather most likely worked and where he later helped organize labor unions so that workers (including himself) could work in better, safer conditions and give their families better lives. I also stood in front of the German Lutheran school that my mother attended. It is no longer a private school and Lutheran church but is now a church that serves the African American community in the neighborhood. Still, the concrete marker engraved with the school's original name remains.

🏠

My dogs accompany me to the Belle Writer's Studio every day. I take breaks when I need them, not when someone else says I can. If I feel like leaving in the middle of the day to take the dogs for a long walk and returning to work in the middle of the night, I do so. I drink coffee at my desk in mugs that don't have to be approved by anyone but me. (Yes, only corporate-approved mugs could be used at our desks at one of my jobs.) They include one that says, "My journey begins today"; my dog mug that states, "My love is unconditional"; my "Life is good" mug; and the Fleetwood Mac mug I picked up after seeing their concert from a VIP suite on another assignment.

Years ago, this writer's cabin in the woods, my Belle Writer's Studio, was just a dream, with its shelves that hold all of the books I hold dear (including some of my mother's) and its brightly painted yellow walls. I had enough gray to last me a lifetime, and I want to be surrounded by upbeat, happy colors. My cabin doesn't match perfectly what I envisioned two decades ago—it doesn't have that "divorce boat" in front of it—but it's perfect for me.

It all boils down to being able to do *what* I love to do, where I *want* to do it. Many people spend the prime of their lives at jobs that they hate, sometimes at the expense of their mental and physical health. Living Large is about working to live, not living to work. For many in the tiny house movement, that means working from our land.

On the wall across from my desk is a framed copy of my first paid published piece, with a copy of the $25 check I received. The essay is about the wonderful childhood

I had in my neighborhood while growing up. I cashed the check and paid about four times its amount to have the copy framed with the essay.

But it serves as a daily reminder of how far I've come in achieving my dreams. I don't regret my educational path or the time I spent in corporate life. Sometimes the path leads us straight ahead, and sometimes there are a few detours. If we are alert, those detours can show us a lot of scenery we might otherwise not have discovered.

Hard at work in the Belle Writer's Studio.

## Building the Belle Writer's Studio

Working from our 10-by-10-foot bedroom in Our Little House the first year we lived here was akin to working from an airplane seat. My space was so cramped that if my chair swiveled slightly, all my research papers and interview notes would fall on the floor. I was embarrassed to allow anyone into our home, even my new part-time assistant. A file cabinet cluttered the living room, and she had to sit at the tiny kitchen table to work.

When we realized we would be more financially comfortable in Our Little House, I knew we had to do something to make our lives more physically comfortable. As we learned, building on to Our Little House really wasn't an option.

My aunt and I sat down and designed the Belle Writer's Studio using the same computer program we used to design Our Little House. There were some design elements I would have changed at Our Little House if given a second chance, and we were able to incorporate them in the writer's studio. For example, I wanted an open, airy office with a lot of big windows.

We created a tall, cathedral ceiling and added heavy wood beams like those found in rustic lodges. We put in three large windows, one on each of the side walls and one on the back wall so I could look out into our majestic forest while working. However, I kept the front wall free of windows to accommodate a futon and a large piece of art.

Dale and I had numerous discussions about adding a bathroom in the studio. Adding a bathroom with a shower was an additional expense, but it wasn't very practical for me to run 50 yards to the house every time nature called. When we built Our Little House, we had installed a septic tank large enough for a two-bath home, so fortunately we didn't have to put in a new tank. We only had the cost of running the well line and plumbing.

We also wanted to include at least a half-basement to store my interview notes and other important legal documents. Additionally, we needed a storm shelter in which to seek refuge during tornadoes and other severe weather. Luckily, we were able to build a three-quarter basement without blasting rock. We also reinforced the ceiling of the basement to create a storm shelter.

We designed the bathroom in the Belle Writer's Studio with a pocket door. Pocket doors are great space savers because they don't swing out, but slide back into the wall when not in use. It's one of my favorite design features in my office. The bathroom has a door without it taking up any prime wall space.

The pocket door leading to the bathroom in the Belle Writer's Studio.

One of the most important features that we carried over from Our Little House was installing quality, heavy-wear laminate flooring. There isn't a stitch of carpet anywhere on our property, and I will never deal with carpet again. We also decided on a high-efficiency, Energy Star–rated, wall-mounted heat and air unit. I did not want to keep two fires going for warmth in the winter or fight another window air-conditioning unit for the lovely view during the summer.

I also wanted any future owners who might someday remodel the Belle Writer's

Studio to know our history. I wrote a letter telling of our life here and put it in an enve-lope with some photos. I dropped it into a wall of the studio before it was covered with drywall. When I was a kid, I did the same thing when my parents remodeled our little bungalow. I don't remember where I got the idea—maybe from studying letters written during the Civil War—but my mom thought it was a great idea. I've often wondered if any of the owners have remodeled and found my letter, written in a nine-year-old's hand.

I hope no one finds my letter in the Belle Writer's Studio for generations, but who-ever finds it will know the history of the land and how much we loved this place.

Building a new home or a writer's studio isn't always smooth sailing, and running into unforeseen problems when embarking on a construction project isn't uncommon. One of the downsides of building in a very rural area is that the choice of contractors is lim-ited. On both our builds, we were very lucky to have wonderful and talented general contractors, but some of the specialized subcontractors on the Belle Writer's Studio left a lot to be desired.

The plumbing contractor didn't recess the drain in the shower properly, so water stands in the floor of the shower unless it is manually wiped out. The other problem ended up being a literal shitty one. That same contractor failed to cap the sewer line af-ter doing the installation, which caused raw sewage to spew out of the pipe in the crawl space of the basement, rather than traveling to the septic. Luckily, I had to go down to the basement not very long after I started using the toilet in the studio. I'm not sure if I saw the problem first or smelled it, but we got it capped.

Getting the drywall contractor to our property to finish the Belle Writer's Studio also proved to be a task that tested my patience to its limits because he kept putting us off until I threatened to hire someone else. There's a saying around here that "things get done when people get around to it." This is especially true when it seems everyone is operating on "mountain time."

When we first moved here, I met a woman and we became friends. (I was especially lonely during the week as Dale was still in Kansas City for those first few months.) We had lunch a few times, and she warned me about the "mountain time" phenomenon. She and her husband had been living here quite a while by that point (several years, in fact), and her husband hadn't even finished building the inside of the home they had built. They were still living in a house with just studs and plywood floors. She said as soon as they retired from their paying jobs and moved in, her husband had gotten on mountain time himself.

Fortunately, I've found this to be the only real downside of working from a rural paradise (aside from the slow Internet). There are definitely days we would rather be on the lake than doing anything else. But that's what my covered porch is for on the Belle Writer's Studio. At least I can unplug and go outside while writing.

It took about four months and approximately $30,000 to build the Belle Writer's Studio, and it has been worth every penny. It is also a completely separate structure on separate utilities from Our Little House, which provides some tax benefits for a home-based business.

## Making a Living Is Easier When Bills Are Smaller

Tiny house dwellers are typically an adventurous lot, which also makes them good risk-takers when it comes to entrepreneurism. Many not only yearn for the freedom of having a tiny home, but also desire to control their professional lives.

Annelise and Jake Hagedorn are twentysomethings living their dream in a 192-square-foot tiny home, which has living space and a loft bedroom. They also both recently finished graduate school at Penn State University and are starting their PhDs. Annelise is studying rural sociology and Jake is studying hydrogeology. They support themselves through their company, Brevard Tiny House Company, based in North Carolina, which designs and builds tiny homes for others seeking the same lifestyle. The Hagedorns' tiny home stays parked in the backyard of a home in Pennsylvania, where they pay the landowner rent, but the couple commutes to North Carolina to work on their business when they're not in school.

"We found out about tiny homes when we were in college, and Jake had to do a presentation in environmental design," says Annelise. The couple then went to Sri Lanka to teach English. "When we returned from overseas, we decided we wanted to build one to live in while in grad school."

Annelise says they have fielded calls from all age groups interested in building tiny homes. "People in their 50s seem interested, but it is usually people in their 30s who actually buy," she says. Brevard Tiny Homes average about $45,000, some are higher and some lower, based on the square footage and items added.

Annelise and Jake both work from their tiny home, whether it's schoolwork or creating a tiny home for a client. Annelise works from the loft, while Jake works at the dining room table, which is a portable folding table. "When we first moved in, I thought it would be a problem if the light was on downstairs because I'm a morning person and Jake's a night person," says Annelise. "But the table is under the loft, which blocks out most of the light, so it's worked out."

Annelise and Jake Hagedorn are pursuing their PhDs and running the Brevard Tiny House Company from their 192-square-foot home.

One thing Annelise has found challenging is climbing into the loft with a laptop, books, and cell phone in hand. "It's really a juggling act," she says. Fortunately, there haven't yet been any disasters involving electronics dropped from the loft.

Overall, the tiny lifestyle works smoothly for the young couple. Annelise says that living abroad taught them how to live in a small space together. "We get along really well, which helps. When we lived abroad, we got food poisoning quite a bit, and when someone is sick, you see things you can't unsee," she says, laughing. "We really just like to hang out with each other."

## How They Make a Living

Many tiny house dwellers have found niches in writing about their experiences on blogs. Hari Berzins (tinyhousefamily.com) and Tammy Strobel (rowdykittens.com) both have successful blogs where they each write about their tiny house lives. Tammy also teaches classes in various writing modalities, such as journaling, as well as photography. Hari and Karl Berzins teach an online course in debt-free living, in addition to consulting and helping design and build tiny homes for others. Diane Selkirk is a successful writer and photographer who writes travel and other articles about her family's life on the sea.

Other tiny home dwellers make a living or supplement their income by living off of the land. Mary Dunning has a goat-milk-soap business, and Ariel McGlothin uses food from her garden to cook healthy meals that she barters for rent and other services.

Some tiny house dwellers supplement their income by becoming landlords. Vicki Salmon says that after moving to their slightly larger dream log cabin, they are renting out their first tiny cabin, which is an option for anyone who wants to build more than one tiny home on their property. "We are currently renting it out for $650 per month," says Vicki. "We could get more, but we're only renting it out to friends and family, so we don't want to charge them market rate."

Others, such as Aaron and Alyson Courain, hope to build and operate a tiny house hotel.

Ramona and Carlo DeAngelus still own their former larger homes, but they plan on selling his and paying hers off and renting it out, which will generate income.

## **LIVING LARGE TIPS:** Establishing a Home-Based Business

- Do what you know or have a passion for. Living Large is all about living our passions, whether at work or play. If you're good at designing websites, helping companies with their social-media marketing, or writing proposals for a corporation, maybe you could do it from your home.

- Research your endeavor. Talk to others who are in business; find out what you should avoid; learn what's hot in your field.

- Even if you don't plan on taking out a business loan, speak with a small-business incubator (sometimes located on local college campuses) and get help writing a business plan. This helps give you a map of where you are going before you start.

- Build up some savings before quitting your day job. It can take months to turn a profit in a new business.

# 15

# Hindsight Is 20/20:
## Ensuring Your Living Large Future

*Living Truth:* "*Hindsight is wonderful. It's always very easy to second guess after the fact.*"

**—HELEN REDDY**

Let's review key points. Living a "sustainable life" isn't just about protecting the environment and planet. It's also about building what you need now and what you will need in the future, so you can have a sustainable, long-term home.

Our journey to Our Little House was unconventional, as it was really my mom, aunt, and uncle who chose where they were going to live and then part of the land was given to us. We then became accidental full-time little house dwellers. Hopefully, your journey might be a little more planned out. If it is, choosing the right home style and place for your Living Large dream should be your first step.

When we built Our Little House, we knew we wanted a home on a foundation, not a tiny house on a trailer or an RV. This is important to decide before choosing your location. In many jurisdictions, the building codes and laws have not caught up with the mobile little house movement. While rural areas generally have more relaxed building codes regarding minimum square footage requirements, some will not allow mobile homes that aren't hooked up to a permanent water source or that don't have a septic sewer system (in other words, no composting toilets).

Be sure to check your state laws if you are building a mobile tiny home. Some states require tags and registration on all trailers, while some only require them if the trailer and its load are above certain weight. Qualified small homebuilders should be able to help you navigate the various codes and building restrictions in your area.

When my mom, aunt, and uncle found our property in 1984, they spotted it in the classifieds sections of a rural-living magazine. These are still good places to search for available land. Nowadays, the Internet makes it easy to find a qualified real estate agent in the area where you are looking to buy.

A little-known benefit of settling on previously uninhabited land is that some states still give a homesteading credit—a tax break—for personal property taxes. Extremely rural areas sometimes offer the homesteading credit as a way to increase their population. They may be giving up $300 in property taxes, but they hope to gain revenue through sales tax and licenses on vehicles, boats, trailers, and recreational vehicles.

A word of caution: Never purchase a piece of property without first seeing it in person. When we purchased our adjoining 6.9 acres of property just before we moved here, we bought it from a young man who had inherited it from his parents. They had purchased the land in 1974, sight unseen, and they had been told that the property was "lakefront," which it isn't.

When the young man quoted us a price, we told him he was asking way too much. He sent us proof that the seller had told them that their land was lakefront and that they had purchased it for well over the market value at the time. (They paid more per acre than my family did in 1984 for land that is actually lakefront.) We proved the 2007 market value and negotiated with him to that asking price, which was barely more than what his parents had paid in 1974.

When looking at a piece of property, it is also a good idea to check with the county or township, and gather as much information that you can about it. Was it ever occupied? Who owned it, and what was it used for? Sometimes properties have hidden environmental concerns. Also, have an appraiser tell you if you've been quoted a good deal, and have a builder, if possible, give you an opinion on building possibilities for the site. For example, if your little home is going to require a septic system, the soil has to be able to "perc" (handle the waste) before it can be built.

Also keep in mind that, even if a property is very rural when you purchase it, this may not always be the case. Aunt Kathy told me many times how, when they came to look at the property in 1984, the real estate agent told them that the land was so far off the beaten path that it would never be developed.

"Good," she said they told him. "That's exactly what we want."

The dirt road was little more than a path, and there weren't electrical or telephone lines on the road yet. Aunt Kathy and Monty had to pay the electrical and phone companies to run those lines when they finished their main house.

My, how things have changed. Our end of the road—about a one-mile stretch—has gone from having no homes to having six. All the undeveloped land along the road belongs to private property owners. No one could have foreseen 30 years ago that this area would become a desirable building spot. Our road has become so busy within the past eight years that we now worry about the dogs getting hit by cars.

Living in a rural area on a lake has many advantages. Our lake is owned by the U.S. Corps of Engineers, which means public property surrounds us on all sides. It could be a problem if rabble rousers wanted to party on the lakeshore, but it is only typically a problem for us during hunting season. We've had a few minor run-ins with hunters who don't stay off marked private property.

It's a good idea, if you're buying adjacent to public lands, to check into what is and isn't allowed near your property. We had no idea that steel-jawed traps were allowed on the lakeshore until one of Aunt Kathy's dogs was caught in one. Fortunately, the dog survived.

Laws can change after you purchase a piece of property. The lot that my parents purchased on a lake in Kansas ended up being worthless as a building spot. After my parents purchased the lot, the town enacted new regulations requiring owners who want to build a home to have two lots in order to have room for a septic system. In addition, the bylaws of the lake forbid mobile structures. Therefore, a mobile tiny house with a composting toilet or even an RV could not be placed on my parents' lot. Since neither neighbor on each side (who built their homes before the new rules were put into place) was interested in purchasing the lot, my mom stopped paying taxes on it, and to my knowledge, it went to the county.

Many jurisdictions grandfather in old regulations for people who purchase prior to a new law, but some don't. It's wise to stay up on any changing regulations in a jurisdiction where you've purchased property but not yet built a house.

In other words, builder beware. Talk to local officials about any plans for the surrounding property and how it's zoned. For example, a large piece of property one cove over from ours is currently zoned for a major park and resort. If this is ever built, it will greatly affect our quality of life.

## You Have Your Land: Designing Your Tiny House

I talked about building the right-size home for you family in Chapter 3. Although we didn't know Our Little House would be our permanent residence when we built it, we designed it as a fully functioning home, where two people would be comfortable for as long as necessary.

It has a bathtub that I can't live without, full-size appliances in the kitchen, and a washer and dryer. These are all things you have to think about when designing your little home for the long term.

Some tiny homes on trailers are built with composting toilets and have only showers, and they have to be hooked up to a water source. Many people find they don't mind going to the gym to shower in the winter or having a composting toilet. They are fine with not having four burners on the stove or not having a full-size refrigerator or oven.

However, other folks find they've gone too small when it comes to tiny house living. Carrie and Shane Caverly, who own Clothesline Tiny Homes (clotheslinetinyhomes. com), moved out of their tiny home after 18 months. Carrie wrote on her blog that the house was just too tiny and didn't fit their needs. She wrote that she could probably live in a tiny home if she were single. She indicated that they didn't have any privacy, office space, room for yoga, or storage. They moved from their tiny home into what she described on the blog as a "full-size home." They've bought a piece of property, where they plan on eventually building a home under 1,000 square feet and living debt-free.

One thing Dale and I struggled with when we built Our Little House was whether to put up a wall between the bedroom and living room. The wall makes the two rooms smaller, and the standard bedroom door takes up valuable wall space in the bedroom. (Again, check into pocket doors, they are awesome!) But Dale likes to stay up late while I'm typically an early-to-bed, early-to-rise type. We also wanted to provide some privacy in case we had guests. (We have a futon that folds into a full-size bed in the living room.) So, we opted for the wall.

Another choice I'm glad we made was to build the house with the best possible materials that we could afford. We built it using 2-by-6 beams, instead of the 2-by-4 that codes required. This means the beams are larger, which allows room between the walls for more insulation. Since all our plumbing is on outside walls, we had our contractor put extra insulation in, particularly around the pipes.

This made our house so airtight that condensation builds up on the wooden windows in the winter. We put in good, energy-efficient windows that tilt in for easy cleaning, but with the condensation buildup, we have to be careful to keep them clear of mold by scrubbing them often, a problem that Ariel McGlothin has dealt with in her tiny home as well.

Even though it takes up valuable space, we're glad for the extra privacy that the wall between our bedroom and living room gives us.

There is less room for air to circulate in a tiny house, so this is a common problem. Mold can be potentially dangerous to your health and can cause allergies and other health problems. When designing your house, you need to plan good ventilation. You can install a ceiling fan in your bathroom to help vent steam when you're in the shower or bath. Also, install a good range hood in your kitchen that has ductwork to the outside, as opposed to a ductless fan, which just reroutes air and humidity through a filter and back into your little house.

It's important to have separate fans so that the humidity in your kitchen is not sucked throughout the house to your bathroom and visa versa. If you've already built your tiny home and didn't plan for good ventilation, you can still add it or at the very least, add a dehumidifier to reduce the probability of mold.

Good doors and windows are an excellent investment; if you don't put these in during construction, you'll likely end up having to replace them. Sue Smith Moak says although she and Rick put in double-pane windows when they built their small cabin, they weren't the best of quality and she had to replace the windows the spring after Rick passed away. "The seals were starting to crack, so I ordered custom triple-pane windows," says Sue. "They also tilt in, so that will keep me off the ladder outside."

🏠

Dale and I plan on living in Our Little House for a long time. If this is going to be your home during retirement and you're hoping to stay in it for the rest of your life, give serious consideration to building using Universal Design, a method of building that allows for people in wheelchairs to have access everywhere in the house. The doors and walkways are wider, the cabinets are lower, and the tub/shower is built to be accessible.

Universal Design does cost more, and it is something I wish we had done in Our Little House. (I was hoping to incorporate it into the future larger house that didn't happen.) Using it in a little house may require adjusting the layout of your home to accommodate the larger doorways and pathways, but the cost and adjustments will be well worth it should you want to stay in your home as long as you wish.

There are many things to take into consideration when choosing the tiny house lifestyle. Don't rush. Take your time in deciding where you want to live and how big of a home you need—and do *lots* of research. It may take some trial and error, but you'll know in your heart when you're truly Living Large.

# Epilogue

I awoke with a jolt, as I had so many times in the years since I locked the door for the last time to the Wilson House. That home was my mother's dream, but it was the setting of a recurring nightmare for me. In those night terrors, the house was much larger than the 1,800 square feet it was in reality, and the attic access led to a secret room on the top floor of the house with a dark monster.

The nightmare was part of the clutter that followed me from house to house for years, and it was even haunting my sleep at Our Little House. Was it, as my mom had thought, the remnants of teenage angst from living in our town's rumored haunted abode? Or was it the guilt I felt for not being able, as a 20-year-old college student, to help my mom hang onto her dream home? The answer was something else entirely, one I would not find until a few years into living at Our Little House.

Living in Our Little House has taught me some important lessons about myself. I have realized that my mom losing the Wilson House affected my view of life dreams, burdening me with some of my fears of the future. That single event affected me so greatly that I even mourn a little when friends and loved ones sell homes they once considered their "dream homes."

A couple of years ago, my sister-in-law, Jennifer, fell in love with Phillip, a man she had dated in high school. I was surprised to learn that his family had moved into the Wilson House around the same time my mom sold it. That note I left for the new owners may have well been for his mother. I was very happy to hear Phillip's stories about the home and learn that his family also made good memories there.

Phillip's story made me recognize that many dreams were born and grew in that house, even after my mom's was lost. I had viewed my mom giving up the Wilson House through the lens of loss for so long that I had never focused on the idea that where one family's dream had ended, another's had begun. Whether that note was for Phillip's mom or not (we're not sure as he doesn't remember the year they moved in), what matters is that I now recognize that more happy memories were created in the Wilson house after we were gone.

The other thing I recognize now is my unhealthy attachment to stuff. When we moved to Our Little House, it was as much about running away from my grief as it was embracing our lake-life dream. I mistakenly thought that leaving behind our hometown would help relieve the loss I had felt throughout my adult life. The loss of my dad, the loss of my family home, the loss of friends and loved ones who drifted away, and finally, the loss of my mother.

Instead, by bringing physical reminders of that loss by hauling most of my mom's possessions with us—including things that were bought for and prominently displayed in the Wilson House—I was still clinging to that past. More stuff doesn't help memories live on; if anything, it clutters them.

Finally, since moving to Our Little House, Dale and I survived the worst financial crisis of our marriage. My mom and dad's experiences instilled in me a deep fear of financial difficulties. Thankfully, some of the lessons I learned from their experience—such as not financially overextending ourselves in a large home—helped us through ours. I don't fear such a crisis again because I know our own choices will help us get through it.

That monster in my nightmares didn't represent some fictional boogey man left over from living in the town's haunted house or guilt of not having been able to do something so that my mom could keep her dream home. That monster represented the emotional baggage of those fears passed from my parents and the grief and loss that began the night my dad died. I carried all of that with me throughout my entire adult life.

I transferred that emotional baggage to what remained of my parents' material possessions and connected it to my own fears of what the future might hold. Since I let go of that baggage, I let go of the monster. He no longer plagues my dreams.

I think now of that last evening in our empty dining room in the Wilson House and how the sun highlighted those dust particles riding on that sunbeam. Like that dust, my family scattered in more ways than one on that hot night in July 1984, forever changed. Change is a part of life. Nothing remains the same, like the band Kansas says in their song, "Dust in the Wind."

Now, all that remains of those dust particles are love and memories. I have a lot of both. Sometimes, trying to hold on only holds us back. Letting go of the baggage of the past—both physically and mentally—living simply, embracing loved ones, and following our own dream in Our Little House have helped me recognize this.

I'm looking forward, not back, and I'll never stop believing in what it really means to Live Large.

## A Reaffirmation That We're Home

In the summer of 2015, a good friend of Dale's knew of a job opening for a diesel mechanic and asked if we had any desire to move back to Kansas City.

We love Our Little House, but we had been unable to make substantial headway in the debt we incurred during the recession, nor had we been able to catch up on saving for retirement. Instead of putting my newfound trust that everything will be all right into practice, I began to allow that monster—the fear of financial instability—to control our decisions once again. So, once Dale interviewed for the job and learned it paid substantially more than what he was currently making—with the potential for a lot of overtime—we made the decision to move back to our hometown until we could retire back to Our Little House.

Or, at least we thought we had.

The process of finding a new job was easy compared to the process of finding a place to live. We learned quickly that no one would rent to us since we have multiple dogs. Of course, since our long-term plans involved moving back to Our Little House in 10 years or so, we didn't want to sell it or any of our property.

When we began looking for homes to buy in Kansas City, we couldn't find any in our price range. As Dale pointed out, everything we looked at was like a used car; it seemed they had a lot wrong with them, either aesthetically or structurally, or both.

Dale accepted the job, moved up to the city, and stayed with his sister, Jennifer, for eight weeks while we continued to search for an affordable home in a jurisdiction where we could have all of our dogs. He commuted the 300 miles to Our Little House on the weekends.

As it turns out, not being able to find a house right away was the best thing that could have happened. Dale's new job was located outside of the city, and he was able to test-drive a long commute on busy highways. We were also both able to test-drive how we really felt about moving "home."

From the start of the eight-week experiment, we truly learned to appreciate what we have here: a cozy little home we designed and built. We know every nook and cranny, and we know it doesn't have major structural issues.

We love our "neighborhood" of trees and wildlife, and the humans who are here are spaced far enough apart so that we all have room to ourselves. Dale's commute to work from here might be long and sometimes treacherous in the winter, but he doesn't have to sit in traffic for an hour if there is a wreck on the highway.

Dale was happy with his job and his co-workers here. It may not pay what the job did in the city, but after learning that the overtime wouldn't be what he thought at his new job and our having to increase the price range in houses we were looking at, he would be making about the same in the city.

Most importantly, when we both were in Kansas City, trying to imagine what it would really feel like to live there again, we realized it really no longer felt like "home."

Dale was offered his old job back here near Our Little House, and this is where we plan to stay. We still miss the friends and family we left behind in KC, but as the old adage says—at least for us—it's true that you can never go home again. Kansas City will always be our hometown, and we may not be as financially secure as we'd like to be, but we're truly secure in the knowledge that Our Little House is our home.

# An Update on Our Living Large Families

Of the Living Largers profiled in this book, perhaps the biggest life change happened to **Sue Smith Moak.**

Sue has always been a tough, country-type woman, but she has had to learn to do a lot of things around the property that Rick would have done, such as handle a chain saw, mow the lawn, and manage an assortment of other chores that were usually on her husband's list of "to-dos." To help her adjust, Sue spent a weekend at a women's retreat that was designed to help females tackle tasks typically left to men.

Sue intends to stay at the Rockin RS Ranch and added a bedroom and another bath to bring the total square footage to 808. Sue hopes this will bring her adult children and grandchildren out for visits more often. Although she has the bunkhouse, extended family still had to camp out on the floor of the main cabin when the family gathered altogether. Sue also says the bathroom will allow her a tub, which she has missed.

Sue is also planning for the possibility that she will not be able to live out her entire life on the secluded ranch property. She built another tiny home (an "accessory dwelling") on a foundation on her daughter and son-in-law's property in the Austin, Texas, area. The tiny, 280-square-foot home was built by Kanga Room Systems. Sue's a very rustic, rural-cabin type, but she is going with a modern cabin design in order for the home to fit in more with her daughter's home and neighborhood.

Sue says that there is a lot of discussion in Austin about codes with regards to tiny homes used as accessory dwelling units. In order to comply with current codes in the city, Sue had to remove the kitchen from her tiny house plan. In order to have a kitchen, she would have had to hire an engineer, pay more city fees, and pay a additional plumbing expense of $7,000 to $10,000. Leaving the kitchen out classified the tiny house as an accessory dwelling unit rather than an accessory unit and made the plan more affordable for her budget. Since Sue doesn't stay there often, they put it up for rent on Airbnb, giving people who visit the Austin area a nice alternative to a hotel. It also gives people a chance to try out a tiny home.

Sue has learned a lot about love and loss in the past months since Rick's passing, but she is also learning to carry on and plan for a future she did not foresee when she and Rick dreamed of retiring on their acreage. Sue is continuing to Live Large by adapting to her new normal.

**Tammy Strobel and her husband, Logan Smith,** who live in Northern California, were happy to go home to their tiny house after living in a larger cottage in Yreka that one winter. Tammy said they learned some lessons about what to look for in a future home. For example, Tammy says the house will need to be in a quieter neighborhood. The cottage they rented for the winter was located near a highway. After returning home, the family did rent an apartment in town the next winter.

Tammy says they are still committed to living *intentionally*, but they now realize that doesn't just depend on how much square footage they have. Tammy says that after losing her father in 2012, she had an epiphany about simple living. "I realized living small simply isn't about the size of my house or whether I can tow it down the highway. It's about making mindful choices that give me freedom, flexibility, and the opportunity to spend time with loved ones," Tammy writes on her blog.

**Connie and Ken Howe** completed their first full year in their tiny home in Washington. They are still busy professionals, and although they could afford to have a huge home again, they wouldn't trade their life for anything. When they were building their tiny house, a relative was also building a home—a 3,500-square-footer. "We visited them this past weekend, and her home is absolutely stunning. But Ken and I were talking on the way home, and we wouldn't trade our tiny house for it," Connie says. "We have grown much closer living in a tiny space. It forces you to interact and spend time together."

**Kevin Kalley and David Currier** did retire to their dream in Hawaii. However, they decided they needed a larger main house in order to accommodate a long-term houseguest. They built a larger home and now rent out their 480-square-foot cottage. Kevin says it can also serve as a caregiver's residence, should one be needed as they grow older.

🏠

**Mary Dunning** is still living in her little home in Missouri and running her soap business.

🏠

**The Berzinses** completed their larger home on their land in rural Virginia. They are looking forward to the next adventure on their little house journey—renting their tiny home to others.

🏠

**Aaron and Alyson Courain** are still enjoying their lakefront property in rural New Jersey. At some point, they would like to move to another mountain town, where they can continue pursuing their love of the outdoors. Alyson says wherever they land, they will definitely choose to be in a little home.

🏠

**Ramona and Carlo DeAngelus** are still "outside doing something awesome!"

🏠

**Annelise and Jake Hagedorn** began their PhD programs in the fall of 2015. They still spend their free time building homes for the growing customer base of Brevard Tiny House Company.

🏠

**Ariel McGlothin** is enjoying her garden and spending her time creating great recipes.

**Misti McCloud and Steven Chrystal** enjoyed their first year in their small condo. After moving from the vacation rental, they went back for the belongings they left in storage, but realized they didn't need most of it. Their plan is to save enough money to move to a warm-weather climate. Misti says they will be able to afford that lifestyle because they aren't spending money on stuff, and they'll always save by living in little homes.

**Jay Shafer** continues to inspire others with his talks at tiny house conferences and gatherings. He also continues to impress the tiny house community with his innovative designs for Four Lights Tiny House Company.

**Vicki and Willie Salmon** enjoyed their first year in their larger log cabin in Alaska. They tried out renting the small cabin on their property, but for now, it is being used as a guest house. Vicki was asked to return as principal of the small village school in the remote community of Chalkyitsik, Alaska, so she commutes home on weekends. Their next project includes building another small home on land they own on Kachemak Bay in Homer, Alaska. Vicki says they will continue their debt-free philosophy. "Dreams happen one small step at a time," she says.

**Diane Selkirk's** adventures with her family continue on the high seas. When she has access to the Internet, she posts on her Facebook page about their adventures, including seeing coconut crabs advancing on their meal on the beach on the Chagos Islands in the Indian Ocean, spotting five sharks near their boat, and helping rescue another boat from being stuck on a reef.

**Jane Mosher** is still Living Large in Canada, some days still not believing how much she loves her little home.

**The Gawtry family** enjoyed another Minnesota summer on the lake in their little house. The twins are amazed at people who live with more than one bathroom. Acquiring another bathroom is a reality Bec says the family will have to face as her twins grow older, but she hopes they can build onto their little house instead of having to buy another.

# Resources

## Blogs about the tiny house life
## or sustainable or rural living

*A Porch of My Own (rockinrsranch.blogspot.com)* Sue Smith Moak began writing about her journey with her husband, Rick, on their ranch in the Texas Hill Country. Since he has passed, she is writing about continuing her life alone in a rural setting.

*Another Tiny House Story (livinginatinyhouse.blogspot.com)* This blog chronicles Jess and Dan, a young couple starting a journey toward a self-sustained lifestyle.

*Becoming Minimalist (becomingminimalist.com)* This blog documents the journey of Joshua Becker, his wife, and their two children. In 2008, the family decided to ditch most of their possessions and lead an intentional life. The blog gives tips on living with only a few things.

*Fy Nyth (fynyth.blogspot.com)* This online journal follows the life of Ariel McGlothin as she lives in her tiny, off-grid house in the mountains of Wyoming. Fy Nyth means "My Nest" in Welsh.

*I Love Tiny Houses (ilovetinyhouses.com)* This is a comprehensive site for tiny house enthusiasts.

*Life in 120 Square Feet (120squarefeet.com)* Laura M. LaVoie is a freelance writer and blogger living in a 120-square-foot cabin with her partner, Matt, and their Sphynx cat, Piglet. The couple hand-built their cabin.

*Little House Living (littlehouseliving.com)* This site has tips on saving money and homesteading, and offers recipes.

*Living Big in a Tiny House (livingbiginatinyhouse.com)* This site focuses on design, construction, and space-saving tips.

*Living Large in Our Little House (livinglargeinourlittlehouse.com)* I founded my blog in 2009 to create a community of people who lived in little homes or who were looking to make the move. The blog chronicles our journey of little house life through stories and homemade recipes. We discuss the ins and outs of Living Large in a small space.

*Mini Motives (minimotives.com)* This is the story of Macy, who lives in her 196-square-foot home with her partner, James, their children, Hazel and James, and their Great Dane, Denver.

*My Amazing Epic Life (rdeangelus.wordpress.com/author/rdeangelus/)* Ramona DeAngelus lives her life to the fullest inside and outside of her tiny home. Follow her journey.

*RelaxShacks (www.relaxshacks.com)* Derek "Deek" Diedricksen writes about all things tiny on this site, including books to buy, conferences and workshops to attend, and how-to pointers. Deek is also a builder and host of HGTV's *Tiny House Builders*.

*Rowdy Kittens (rowdykittens.com)* Tammy Strobel began documenting her quest to simplify her life and has made it her mission to help others do the same. She offers wit and wisdom through her writing, as well as online writing and photography classes.

*Small House Bliss (smallhousebliss.com)* This site is dedicated to showcasing well-designed and interesting little houses of all kinds.

*Small House Society (smallhousesociety.net)* Founded by Gregory Johnson in 2002, the Small House Society is a cooperatively managed organization dedicated to the promotion of smaller housing alternatives, which can be more affordable and ecological.

*Tiny House Blog (tinyhouseblog.com)* Founded in 2007, this one of the longest-running blogs in the movement. It features interesting tiny homes, builders, plans, and designs. Kent Griswold is also the founder of the *Tiny House Magazine*.

*Tiny House Community (tinyhousecommunity.com)* This is a site where tiny house enthusiasts can come together and discuss everything tiny.

*Tiny House Dating (tinyhousedating.com)* Find someone just as passionate as you are about tiny house living.

*Tiny House Family (tinyhousefamily.com)* Hari Berzins blogs about her life with her husband and two small children, who all live mortgage-free in a tiny house. The Berzinses teach an online course on how to achieve a debt-free life, and Karl also builds tiny homes.

*Tiny House for Us (tinyhousefor.us)* This site features a list of tiny houses for sale and for rent.

*Tiny House Gear (tinyhousegear.com)* Looking for gear for your tiny house? This is a resource to find anything you might need.

*Tiny House Hotel (tinyhousehotel.com)* Located in the Alberta Arts District in Portland, Oregon, this caravan-style hotel has six models for rent.

*Tiny House Swoon (tinyhouseswoon.com)* Tickle your imagination and get inspired on this site.

*Tiny House Talk (tinyhousetalk.com)* This site is all about tiny homes, resources, and even offers a newsletter about tiny houses and simple living.

*Tiny House Vacations (tinyhousevacations.com)* Try a tiny house on for size while on vacation. This site has listings from all over the world.

*The Tiny Insider (tinyinsider.com)* A website dedicated to the tiny house movement. The resource section is particular invaluable, offering a listing of tiny house blogs, designers, and builders.

*The Tiny Life (thetinylife.com)* Ryan Mitchell's site is a resource for anyone looking for information on the tiny lifestyle.

*Tiny r(E)volution (tinyrevolution.us)* Andrew Odom co-founded this site in 2009 and it has over 900 posts covering tiny house living.

## Builders who specialize in tiny homes

I have compiled a list of builders that specialize in tiny home construction. This is by no means a complete list, and it is not an endorsement of any of the construction companies listed.

As always, before embarking on a construction project and hiring a contractor, you should personally inspect completed projects by the builder, ask for references, and make sure the builder is licensed, bonded, and insured. Always check to make sure there are no complaints filed with the local Better Business Bureau, as well as with local, county, city, or state agencies.

*Alchemy Architects (www.weehouse.com)* Sustainability is the name of the game for this architectural firm in St. Paul, Minnesota. They incorporate reclaimed and repurposed materials into their designs, and partner with the builders and fabricators to create a harmonious blend of the home with the community.

*Atlas (blakestinyhouse.com)* Atlas advertises unique design concepts such as a full wall of windows, solar panels, and rain-capturing features.

*Karl Berzins (tinyhousefamily.com/consulting)* Karl Berzins—who lives with his wife, Hari, and their two children—knows that there are many moving parts to designing and building a tiny home. He and Hari will consult to help you plan (including helping you work with your local government on codes), design, and build the tiny home of your dreams.

*Blue Sky MOD (blueskymod.com)* Blue Sky, located in Toronto, Canada, believes that the foundation of a great little home is aesthetic appeal and ecological responsibility.

*Brevard Tiny House (brevardtinyhouse.com)* Jake and Annelise Hagedorn founded their tiny house company near Brevard, North Carolina, after building their own. They build different sizes and customize to fit their customers' needs.

*Cavco Industries (cavco.com)* Headquartered in Phoenix, Arizona, this company offers a wide variety of small cabins, modular and manufactured homes, and park model RVs.

*Cedar Ridge Industries (cedaridgeindustries.com)* This Chehalis, Washington–based company custom builds park models to specification, as well as RV and cottage-style modular homes. This is the company that built Connie and Ken Howe's park model home, featured in this book.

*The Cottage Company (cottagecompany.com)* This Langley, Washington–based company focuses on the implementation of "pocket neighborhoods" of cottages and "not-so-big" homes.

*Creative Cottages (creativecottagesllc.com)* This small company based in Freeport, Maine, uses environmentally sensitive building practices to create custom, energy-efficient homes in Maine, New Hampshire, and Massachusetts.

*Cusato Cottages (mariannecusato.com)* Marianne Cusato founded Cusato Cottages in Ocean Springs, Mississippi, to provide traditional designs for affordable housing.

*Division 43 (resourcesforlife.com/docs/item4507)* This micro homebuilder in Portland, Oregon, designs and builds tiny homes using reclaimed materials and sustainable practices.

*DPO Construction (dpoconstruction.com)* This Iowa City–based company is dedicated to building energy-efficient and smaller homes.

*First Day Cottage (firstdaycottage.com)* Based in Walpole, New Hampshire, this company sells all-wood house kits.

*Four Lights Tiny House Company (www.fourlightshouses.com)* Jay Shafer, regarded as one of the pioneers of the movement, is constantly designing and innovating tiny homes. His current design is a home with expandable space. He is located in Cotati, California.

*Global Portable Buildings (globalportablebuildings.com)* These steel-cargo container buildings make great tiny homes, offices, or emergency shelters. Located in Santa Rosa, California.

*Greenbuilders, Inc. (greenbuilders.com)* Located in Sparks, Maryland, this company was founded in 2004 with the primary mission to build sustainable houses.

*Gower Design Group (johngowerdesign.com)* This firm offers stock plans or custom-designed homes in Courtenay, British Columbia, Canada. It is founded on the belief that good house design can be a truly transformative force in peoples' lives and for the greater health of the planet.

*Historic Shed (historicshed.com/cottages-and-home-offices)* This Brooksville, Florida, company offers shed designs that can be finished out to serve as a tiny home, office, or guest house.

*Hobbitat Spaces (hobbitatspaces.com)* This Garrett County, Maryland, company offers healthy, energy-efficient spaces for quality living, using reclaimed, sustainable materials. The homes were also featured on FYI Channel's *Tiny House Nation* Halloween 2014 episode.

*Hornby Island Caravans (hornbyislandcaravans.com)* This company designs and builds caravan-style tiny homes on Hornby Island, British Columbia, Canada. The company's goals are to create homes with warmth and character that use all-natural materials and meet the customers' needs.

*Idea Box (ideabox.us)* This Salem, Oregon, company wants you to think of prefab and modular housing in a new way. Idea Box uses energy- and resource-efficient construction to create affordable, cool, and fun housing.

*Insite Builders (insitebuilders.com)* These steel-construction homes are small, cute, modern, and very strong. The website includes large photos, basic floor plans, and beautiful 3D-model drawings.

*JoT House (jothouse.com)* Based in Los Angeles, California, this company designs and builds small, simple, modern-design little homes.

*Just Cabins (justcabins.co.nz)* Just Cabins operates throughout New Zealand to offer cozy, warm little homes that fit the lifestyle and budget of their customers.

*Kanga Room Systems (kangaroomsystems.com)* These modern modular homes are built in Austin, Texas. There are options on their Cottage Cabin plans, where customers can select wall and flooring finishes, paint colors, and siding packages.

*Lancaster County Barns (lancasterbarns.com)* This Lancaster County, Pennsylvania, company offers small homes, barns, and offices crafted from the finest materials, available in a wide variety of styles, as well as price points.

*Little Green Buildings (littlegreenbuildings.com)* Little Green Buildings was created for people who need a small, earth-friendly, nontoxic, affordable, and easily assembled building. The Port Angeles, Washington, company advertises that their homes can be assembled by just about anyone.

*Little House on the Trailer (littlehouseonthetrailer.com)* This Petaluma, California, company offers factory-built, high-quality, energy-efficient houses. The company starts with an interview to determine your needs and can build a tiny house on a trailer, a park model, or a little home.

*Living Architecture (livingarchitecture.com)* This Cottonwood Shores, Texas, firm says Living Architecture is more than the name of the company. It is also a movement . . . all about living. The company's mission is to design and build sustainable structures.

*M-house (m-house.org)* The homes designed by this London-based company are all about being modern, mobile, meticulous, minimalist, and marvelous.

*Maximus Extreme Living Solutions (maximusextreme.com)* Maximus was founded by Stew MacInnes, who has been a real estate broker in Utah since 1991. The company also has a partner in helping people finance their tiny homes.

*Michigan Tiny Home (mitinyhome.com)* This company produces what they describe as "Amish constructed," American-made tiny homes. Homes can be delivered fully operational, as just the shell on wheels, or stationary-ready for a foundation.

*m-ch (Micro Compact Home: microcompacthome.com)* These homes were developed as an answer to the increasing demand for short-stay accommodations throughout Europe.

*Miles Building and Design (mbdaustin.com)* Roy Miles—owner of this Austin, Texas, company—says his specialty is "using sustainable building practices to create efficient use of space that is tailored to your needs, with a high level of craftsmanship." He claims over twenty years of experience in modern construction using green-building practices, traditional-timber framing, natural-building methods with straw bale and cob, and furniture and cabinet making.

*Mini-Cabin Plans (minicabinplans.com)* Architect and builder Kevin Meek is the provider of this website, which offers unique and inexpensive building plans for low-cost small housing.

*Mini Homes by Sustain (sustain.ca)* This company—based in Toronto, Ontario, Canada—designs little homes, which are created by Altius Architecture and Sustain Design Studio.

*New Avenue Homes (newavenuehomes.com)* Located in San Francisco, California, New Avenue Homes builds homes on underutilized properties within existing neighborhoods. "We have unique expertise in design, land use rights, financing, permitting, and prefab manufacturing that allows us to create building opportunities where it is either illegal or unprofitable for the old-fashioned banks, builders and developers to operate. By creating new legal and financial products we eliminate the barriers that foil the old way of building and enable the creation of tens of thousands of right-sized homes that are energy efficient, attractive and healthy to live in."

*Noble Home (noble-home.net)* This company's goals are to provide inspired, afford-able housing by shipping kits to the home site. "A kit can save labor costs because most pieces are cut to size, therefore assembly is typically very fast. Wasted time and money due to incorrect ordering of materials and complex construction is avoided with a kit." The company is based in Shelburne Falls, Massachusetts, and also offers passive-solar homes.

*Noncompliant Design (noncomdesign.com)* Located in Nordland, Washington, the company says, "Our feature design is ECOSOLO, the culmination and refinement of a building design first sketched on paper nearly thirty years ago. ECOSOLO exhibits a strong focus on material and construction system economics."

*Oasis Design (oasisdesign.net)* Oasis, located in Santa Barbara, California, says its goal is "to help people live healthy, enjoyable, and meaningful lives, by helping get the nuts and bolts of simple, sustainable systems to really work." The company specializes in deep-green, integrated designs for water supply, greywater reuse, edible landscaping, and passive solar.

*Oregon Cottage Company (oregoncottagecompany.net)* This Eugene, Oregon, company strives to provide healthy tiny homes of the highest craftsmanship to a grow-ing demographic of individuals wanting a simpler way of life.

*Portland Alternative Dwellings (PAD) (padtinyhouses.com)* Dee Williams is best known for her book *The Big Tiny*, detailing her tiny house and minimalist journey. This is her Oregon-based company, which constructed Tammy Strobel and Logan Smith's tiny home.

*Pixie Palace Hut Co. (www.shepherdhutsusa.com)* The Shepherd Hut Design may have originated in England, but now it can also be found in Northern Michigan. These homes come with authentic cast-iron wheels forged in England and imported to the United States. Choose your chassis, hut size, and even the positioning of the windows.

*The Q Cabin Kits (theqcabin.com)* These cabin kits are based on green technology and are designed with sustainable micro-housing in mind. "We use steel stud and foam wall panels, natural fibers, high-tech insulation methods, low-E insulated glass, passive and active solar systems, automatic ventilation systems, and sustainable-sized footprints.

The end result is an architecturally pleasing, resource-efficient, and environmentally friendly cabin."

*Rich's Portable Cabins (richsportablecabins.com)* This company is located in Powder, Oregon, but advertises that it can ship its park model homes all over the country. Rich's also has an office in Virginia.

*Rocio Romero LV Series Homes (rocioromero.com/LVSeries.html)* This St. Louis, Missouri, company designs, builds, and ships all of its kit homes. The company also offers custom-built homes.

*Rockhill and Associates (rockhillandassociates.com)* This company is located in Lecompton, Kansas, and offers designs for custom little homes, as well as offices.

*Ross Chapin Architects (rosschapin.com)* Based on Whidbey Island, Washington, this custom architectural firm has been designing scaled homes since 1982. "Our work shows that neighborhoods, buildings, and outdoor spaces can be alive and vibrant, authentic and soulful. We strive to create places that nourish the individual, support positive family relationships, and foster a strong sense of community."

*Sheldon Designs (sheldondesigns.com)* Andy Sheldon, owner of this Skillman, New Jersey, firm, says on his website that he has been designing cabins, cottages, barns, and sheds for over twenty-five years. His mission is to provide "beautiful, economical, easy-to-build designs with complete blueprints at reasonable prices."

*Sing Tiny House (singtinyhouse.com)* The building system offered by this McCleay, Washington, company—founded in 1992—uses Sing honeycomb panels.

*Small House Lab (smallhouselab.com)* Based in New York City, Small House Lab "sells plans and 3D models of prototype small houses, and shares ideas about finding more in less."

*Steven Holl Architects (stevenholl.com)* This design firm, founded in the 1970s, has been creating home designs from its New York City offices and winning awards while doing it.

***Structures To Go (structurestogo.com)*** This company's building kits are manufactured in their Port Angeles, Washington, plant. There are several styles that are lightweight, energy-efficient, environmentally friendly, versatile, and easy to assemble.

***Stiles Designs (stilesdesigns.com)*** Based in New York City and East Hampton, David Stiles is a designer, builder, illustrator, and the author of more than twenty how-to building books.

***Tennessee Tiny Homes (tinyhappyhomes.com)*** These tiny homes are built in Collierville, Tennessee, and are on trailers so that they can be taken anywhere the owner wants to live. They range from 120 to 200 square feet.

***Timberlast (timberlast.com)*** "Timber framing is a post and beam construction that is one of the oldest in the world. For connections, they require joinery that fit together with glove-like precision. These joints rely on the expertise of the builder: No metal fasteners are used to connect the frame together, only precision and pegs." Based in Nottingham, New Hampshire.

***Tiny House Build (tinyhousebuild.com)*** "Andrew Morrison has been a professional builder for twenty years and has been teaching people how to build their own homes in his hands-on workshops since 2004."

***Tiny Portable Cedar Cabins (tinyportablecedarcabins.com)*** This company sells portable cedar cabins on skids or steel trailers that range in size from 144 to 400 square feet. They offer radiant floor heating.

***Tiny Texas Houses (tinytexashouses.com)*** This company—based in Luling, Texas—says it is one of the only tiny house companies in the United States that constructs its homes using 95 percent recycled materials.

***Tortoise Shell Home (tortoiseshellhome.com)*** Located in Calistoga, California, this company offers tiny homes from 120 square feet that can travel with you wherever you go.

*Tumbleweed Tiny House Company (tumbleweedhouses.com)* Likely the most recognized name in the tiny house building industry, Tumbleweed mounted its first tiny house on a trailer in 1999. The company is based in Colorado Springs, Colorado, but they have built tiny houses for homeowners all over the United States.

*Yurts of America (yurtsofamerica.com)* This company boasts that it has one of the most economical and well-built year-round yurts on the market.

**Van Wyk Woodbuilders (vanwykwoodbuilders.com)** This Des Moines, Iowa, husband-and-wife team builds customized cabins using high-quality, hand-picked wood. Cabin sizes range from 8 by 8 to 14 by 24 feet.

*Wee Cabin Company (weecabins.com)* This Mount Shasta, California, company builds handcrafted timber-frame cabins. The company has been in business since 2005 and has been featured in a number of high-profile media outlets such as *Cabin Life* magazine.

*YehStudio (yehstudio.com)* This firm has offices in Los Angeles, California, and Honolulu, Hawaii, and is a full-service design firm. "We are committed to progressive design strategies for the built environment. Our building system is very flexible and can be adapted to cover anything from a small detached studio to a three-bedroom house and up."

## Insurance Agents

*Darrell Grenz, Grenz Insurance Agency (503-206-6736)* Insurance only in limited western states.

*Dave Fleming, RV America Insurance (rvainsurance.com; 800-400-0186)* This is the insurance company that will insure Tumbleweed Tiny House models. Some bloggers have reported that he can help insure models built by others.

# Notes

1. investopedia.com/terms/a/american-dream.asp

2. census.gov/const/C25Ann/sftotalmedavgsqft.pdf

3. statista.com/statistics/183648/average-size-of-households-in-the-us

4. davemanuel.com/median-household-income.php

5. census.gov/const/C25Ann/sftotalmedavgsqft.pdf

6. reuters.com/article/2010/01/14/us-usa-housing-foreclosures-idUSTRE60D0LZ20100114

7. pewresearch.org/daily-number/baby-boomers-retire/

8. census.gov/construction/chars/pdf/medavgsqft.pdf

9. census.gov/construction/chars/highlights.html

10. census.gov/housing/hvs/files/currenthvspress.pdf

11. bloomberg.com/news/2014-04-29/u-s-homeownership-rate-falls-to-the-lowest-since-1995.html

12. credit.com/press-releases/many-americans-debt-free-still-american-dream/

13. huffingtonpost.com/marko-rubel/is-the-tiny-house-market-_b_6882688.html

14. realtormag.realtor.org/daily-news/2014/07/10/tiny-homes-spark-big-movement

15. wric.com/2015/04/06/chesterfield-couple-being-forced-out-of-tiny-dream-home

16. kait8.com/story/28895014/ordinance-to-ban-tiny-houses-goes-before-city-council

17. host.madison.com/news/local/writers/ogechi-emechebe/occupy-madison-s-tiny-houses-village-looking-to-add-more/article_06c271e0-8b1a-50fc-bc89-a0e87d2d9ae4.html

18. twcnews.com/nys/watertown/news/2015/04/23/tiny-homes-homelessness-solution.html

19. wlox.com/story/28886453/waveland-leaders-buy-in-to-tiny-house-concept

20. imdb.com/title/tt0068473/locations?ref_=tt_dt_dt

21. ktar.com/168/1760675/Let-kids-play-outside-alone-It-should-be-a-crime-poll-says

22. money.cnn.com/2008/06/08/news/economy/gas_prices/

23. coolclimate.berkeley.edu/carboncalculator

24. water.usgs.gov/edu/qa-home-percapita.html

25. bostonglobe.com/lifestyle/2015/02/02/why-difficult-make-friends-after/QluddtlCLPxJjz4972R WZM/story.html

26. washingtonpost.com/local/boomers-unwanted-inheritance/2015/03/27/0e75ff6e-45c4-11e4 -b437-1a7368204804_story.html

# Photo Credits

All images in this book are by Kevin Pieper, with the exception of the following:

Title page (left to right): Victoria Salmon, Misti McCloud, Ken and Connie Howe, Rebecca Gawtry, Nick Sloff, Kevin Pieper, Ariel McGlothin, Alicia R. Mainer

2, 3 (right), 6 (right), 11, 13, 15, 16, 24, 37, 92, 114, 144, 160: Kerri Fivecoat-Campbell
3 (left), 6 (left), 7: Angela Henderson Eldering
31: Occupy Madison
41: Misti McCloud
42: Kevin Kalley
44, 89: Rebecca Gawtry
46, 47, 97 (bottom right), 150: Tammy Strobel/rowdykittens.com
48, 49, 97 (bottom left), 105: Ken and Connie Howe
60, 112, 148, 166: Sue Smith Moak
63, 73, 88, 138: Karl and Hari Berzins
75, 97 (top right), 124: Ariel McGlothin
84: Jodine Baluk
85, 169: Diane Selkirk
86, 106, 123, 165: Alicia R. Mainer
97 (top left), 145, 146, 149, 167: Aaron Courain and Aly Courain
127: Victoria Salmon
168: Steve Chrystal
179: Nick Sloff

# Index

# About the Author

**Kerri Fivecoat-Campbell** is a journalist and author who has written a column on small space living for Parade.com. She's also written on small space living for *Mother Earth News* and Realtor.com and has been interviewed extensively on her tiny house expertise. Her work has also appeared in *Audubon Magazine, Entrepreneur Magazine,* Yahoo! News, MSN.com and NBC Digital's pet channel. A member of the American Society of Journalists and Authors, the Society of American Travel Writers, and the Society of Environmental Journalists, a past national board member of the Society of Professional Journalists, and a past president of the Kansas City Press Club, Kerri's other writing specialties includes animals and pets, business, travel, and the environment. She loves boating and fishing, hiking, and spending time with her husband of 30 years and their dogs. Kerri lives an intentional life with an eye toward sustainability in a 480-square-foot cabin in the Ozark Mountains with her husband and five "recycled" (rescue) mutts, which she documents on her blog, Living Large in Our Little House.